THE BARBECUE LOVER'S BIG BOOK OF BBQ SAUCES

THE BARBECUE

225 Extraordinary Sauces, Rubs,

LOVER'S

Marinades, Mops, Bastes, Pastes, and

BIG BOOK OF

Salsas, for Smoke-Cooking or Grilling

BBQ SAUCES

CHERYL AND BILL JAMISON

The Harvard Common Press | Boston, Massachusetts

The Harvard Common Press
www.harvardcommonpress.com

Printed in China
Printed on acid-free paper

Library of Congress Cataloging-in-Publication Data
Jamison, Cheryl Alters.
  The barbecue lover's big book of BBQ sauces : 225 extraordinary sauces, rubs,
marinades, mops, bastes, pastes, and salsas, for smoke-cooking or grilling /
Cheryl and Bill Jamison. -- First edition.
      pages cm
  Includes index.
  ISBN 978-1-55832-845-7 (acid-free paper)
  1. Barbecuing. 2. Barbecue sauce. I. Jamison, Bill. II. Title.
  TX840.B3J339 2015
  641.7'6--dc23

                    2014041185

Special bulk-order discounts are available on this and other Harvard Common Press books.
Companies and organizations may purchase books for premiums or resale, or may arrange
a custom edition, by contacting the Marketing Director at the web address above.

BOOK AND COVER DESIGNER: *Richard Oriolo*
PHOTOGRAPHER: *Gabriella Marks*
CHEF DE LIVRE: *Mike Whistler*

10 9 8 7 6 5 4 3 2 1

FOR ALL OUR FAMILY AND FRIENDS,

WHO ADD THE SPICE TO OUR LIVES

CONTENTS

PUTTING THE SPICE INTO LIFE

In his epic science-fiction novel *Dune*, Frank Herbert in 1965 envisioned a future in which "He who controls the spice controls the universe." Herbert speaks of a particular fictional spice, but his words ring true today in a broader sense. In our twenty-first-century universe, it's open season on seasonings.

Just two decades ago, when we wrote *Smoke & Spice*, our first outdoor cookbook, many American home cooks seldom ventured beyond salt, pepper, mustard, and ketchup for seasoning food cooked outdoors. Jerk was beginning to catch on, but it was still a newfangled notion. Our range of flavoring options was pretty much limited to what the neighborhood Safeway or Piggly Wiggly stocked.

One expert, John Beaver of Oakland's fabulous Oaktown Spice Shop, reckons that the current universe of seasonings has multiplied many times over since then. Almost anything used anywhere in the world is on our doorstep today, sold even in some chain groceries and always in specialty stores and on the Internet.

In addition to individual spices and other flavoring ingredients, purveyors also peddle numerous packaged blends intended to enable a cook to quickly and easily prepare a dish. Some of these commercial sauces, spice rubs, and other products are quite tasty, but buyers must beware. Many manufactured goods rely heavily on salt and sugar, skewing food flavor instead of enhancing it. It's nearly always better, cheaper, and more fun to put together your own signature creations, as we hope to inspire you to do with our recipes.

TAILORING SEASONINGS TO THE FOOD AND COOKING METHOD

WE TAKE A DIFFERENT approach with our recipes than most books on this subject. After many years of experimenting, we feel strongly that outdoor seasonings should be fine-tuned to what they are flavoring. A concoction that works great on a pork dish won't necessarily taste equally right on a hamburger, chicken breast, or ear of corn. So we've put the focus on the food being cooked rather than the seasoning method, reversing the approach taken by conventional cookbooks. Instead of separate chapters on presumably all-purpose marinades, rubs, bastes, sauces, and other condiments, we have organized the chapters to focus on the meat, poultry, seafood, or produce you are grilling or smoking.

Some seasonings do a fine job on different foods, as we note in the recipes, but every primary ingredient boasts a special affinity for a particular flavor profile. Pork, the most traditional of barbecue-smoked meats, benefits better than other foods from classic barbecue flavors, including both the tangiest and sweetest blends. Because of its assertive inherent taste, beef should be seasoned simply but boldly, and usually in a savory rather than a sweet fashion. Poultry perks up smartly from dry and wet rubs applied under the skin, while seafood has something of a split personality, sometimes favoring a delicate touch and other times a heavier hand. Fruits and vegetables both like a gentle lick of fire and some woodsy smokiness.

Our recipes rely on these underlying principles, but no one should take them as absolute dogma. We don't do that and you shouldn't either. If you find an herbal blend in the lamb chapter that you want to try on pork tenderloin, go for it.

The same applies to our guidance in the recipes about whether a particular seasoning works best for traditional barbecued meats, other foods smoked in a more contemporary style, or grilled dishes. Many cookbooks ignore this distinction, suggesting instead that their sauces, rubs, marinades, and other preparations are suitable for any kind of cooking method. To us, there is an immense difference in the flavor of smoked and grilled foods, which means that they should often be seasoned in different ways. We developed our recipes with this point in mind and always indicate what we intend as the most appropriate use; each recipe has a notation that specifies one or more of these uses: *traditional barbecue, contemporary smoked food*, or *grilled dishes*. If you're in a contrarian mood, just follow your own instincts.

THE MANY WAYS TO ADD FLAVOR TO OUTDOOR FOOD

IN THE RECIPE CHAPTERS, we categorize seasonings according to when they are introduced in the preparation process—that is, before, during, or after the cooking. In the past, most outdoor cooks counted on finishing sauces as the key to flavor, minimizing accents added in advance or at the time of cooking. This works well in some cases, but it can also be a one-dimensional approach. In many situations, what you do before lighting the fire—through the application of a dry spice rub, a paste, or a marinade—can contribute significantly to your results.

Mixtures of dry seasonings massaged onto food, rubs add robust flavors quickly. Allow the spices to meld on your meat or other chow for a little time to concentrate their impact and form a crust. We seek out coarse ingredients when feasible to give greater texture to the crust—for example, using cracked peppercorns and kosher salt or coarse sea salt (also purer and more flavorful than regular table salt). If a recipe calls for dried herbs, resist any temptation you might have to substitute a fresh version, which in this case can compromise taste and texture.

Sometimes called wet rubs, pastes are similar to rubs in nature and effectiveness, but include liquid as well as dry ingredients and don't produce the same crusting effect. They do spread easily, however, making them more adaptable for use in hard-to-reach areas, such as under poultry skin.

Completely liquid, marinades usually impart a subtler touch than other advance seasonings and require more time on food to have an impact. They do not, contrary to lingering myths, keep lean ingredients moist during cooking or tenderize tough cuts. Some food professionals believe that marinades don't do anything, but we disagree. We find them particularly useful for adding flavors that come in liquid form, such as soy sauce and red wine.

Some cooks employ other liquid-based techniques for precook seasoning, including brining and injecting fluids. We've tried both methods numerous times, and have in the past recommended injections, but we have grown skeptical of their value in both cases. Brines are intended to keep lean foods juicy, but they do that by pumping them up with salt water. We won't buy meats treated that way in a grocery store to add weight, so why would we do it at home? The same concern applies to injections, which add moisture as well. Neither technique is necessary to retain juiciness. Mostly they mask flaws in the cooking process. If you grill or barbecue properly, the food will be fine.

For seasoning during the cooking, liquids come into play again in the category of "Mops and Bastes." Likely the oldest of all outdoor flavoring methods, mops are widely used in traditional barbecuing over wood fires to reinforce seasoning that was added earlier with a rub or marinade, or to add new flavor accents. Pitmasters have slathered everything from vinegar to butter over meat for centuries. Bastes serve a similar purpose in grilling and can also be used to keep lean foods moist.

When you're through cooking and ready to eat, you may want to introduce other flavors with a sauce to spread over the food or a special seasoning condiment to serve with it. Our recipes feature a wide range of sauces, including many classic barbecue styles from around the country, as well as plenty of tasty temptations from other corners of the world. Any of them that you adopt for yourself or adapt to your taste will be better than something grabbed from a grocery store shelf.

The "Other Condiments for Flavoring" section of each chapter covers less customary but equally enticing ways to dress your food. We've sifted through the global pantry to find relishes, salsas, chutneys, and more that enhance American outdoor dishes, often in delightfully unexpected ways.

Any of these seasoning techniques can be used on its own or in combination with others. It's fine to stick with a paste or sauce alone on straightforward grilled foods. When we're smoking meat for long hours, we like to build layers of flavor—perhaps with a dry rub, a mop, and a relish—looking always for complementary tones among the various elements. Whatever approach you take, just remember to show off your spicy side.

IMPECCABLE
PORK

DRY RUBS, PASTES, AND MARINADES

SWEET BRUNETTE RUB

FOR TRADITIONAL BARBECUE & CONTEMPORARY SMOKED FOOD

This rub riffs off the revered combo of ham and red-eye gravy. The dark, sultry seasoning is a bit too stout for grilled foods or something small like a smoked pork chop, but the blend pairs beautifully with big cuts of barbecued pork. Rub this into pork shoulder or racks of spare ribs, or pat it over a cooked grocery store ham before giving it a second dose of smoke in the backyard. If you plan to mop your meat, pair this with Sweet Coffee Sop (page 31). For the fullest shot of joe, serve at the table with Sweet Coffee-Cascabel Sauce (page 39). If you'd rather have a contrasting but complementary taste at the table, try Pickled Red Onions (page 54). **MAKES ABOUT 2 CUPS**

> 1 cup dark-roasted coffee beans
> 1/2 cup whole black peppercorns
> 1/4 cup turbinado sugar
> 1/4 cup kosher salt or coarse sea salt
> 1 tablespoon ground dried mild red chile, such as New Mexican or ancho

1. COMBINE all of the ingredients in a coffee or spice grinder, in batches if necessary, and grind them together coarsely.

2. SPRINKLE the rub heavily on the pork and then massage it well into the meat. Allow the seasoned meat to sit for at least 45 minutes at room temperature, or up to overnight wrapped or covered in the refrigerator, prior to cooking.

3. STORE any remaining rub in a covered container in a cool, dark pantry and use within a week for the fullest flavor.

spicing **TIP** **When we make a distinction between "traditional barbecue" and "contemporary smoked food," as we do in the accompanying recipe, we're referring primarily to the length of the smoking process. Traditional barbecue meats such as pork shoulder and spare ribs must be cooked "slow and low" for many hours, sometimes a full day, both to tenderize the tough meat and to achieve optimum smoke flavor. Naturally tender cuts like pork chops or tenderloin, or a precooked ham or sausage (which never were real barbecue meats), need much less time to absorb a smoky taste and don't require a "slow and low" approach for tenderizing. We characterize these and similar fixings as "contemporary smoked foods," even when they are cooked in the same smoker at the same temperature as the world's largest pork shoulder.**

MAPLE SUGAR–CARDAMOM RUB

Maple sugar results from cooking away every bit of moisture from maple sap or syrup. Lots of "experts" will try to convince you that it's healthier for you than other forms of sugar. We choose it, however, in this rub and in other seasonings because of the intense maple aroma and flavor. Be sure to buy the granulated variety of the sugar rather than the powdered, which is intended to melt away when mixed into frostings or butters. Cardamom's exquisite flavor is too elusive to hold up well to long hours of barbecuing, but the briefer smoke-cooking time perfect for pork chops or tenderloin, or for grilling pork, allows the rub to bloom with a citrusy floral note. This recipe should be made up in small quantities because cardamom loses most of its punch quickly after grinding. The sugar content is rather high for a grilling dry rub, so keep the fire in the medium heat range, which is best for many pork cuts anyway. **MAKES ABOUT 3/4 CUP**

> 2 tablespoons green cardamom pods
> 1/2 cup granulated maple sugar
> 2 tablespoons kosher salt or coarse sea salt
> 1 teaspoon freshly grated nutmeg

1. POUR the cardamom pods into a mortar and crush the pods lightly until the black seeds have been released from the hulls. Pick out the bigger pieces of hull (you can leave anything tiny) and discard them. Grind up the black seeds. Mix the ground cardamom with the remaining ingredients.

2. SPRINKLE the rub heavily on pork chops or tenderloin and then massage it in well. Allow the seasoned meat to sit for at least 30 minutes at room temperature, or up to 2 hours wrapped or covered in the refrigerator, prior to cooking.

3. STORE any remaining rub in a covered container in a cool, dark pantry and use within a few days.

BURNING DESIRE DRY RUB

FOR TRADITIONAL BARBECUE

Authentic barbecued pork shoulder, butt, or picnic, or any type of ribs, stands up to a rich mix of chiles. We like to keep a good batch of this fiery rub around most of the year. MAKES ABOUT 1¹/₂ CUPS

1/2 cup ground dried mild to medium red chile, such as New Mexican

1/4 cup ground dried ancho chile

1/4 cup mild sweet paprika

2 tablespoons ground dried pasilla chile

2 tablespoons kosher salt or coarse sea salt

2 tablespoons turbinado sugar

1 tablespoon ground dried chipotle chile

1 tablespoon ground cumin

1 tablespoon freshly ground black pepper

1. STIR together all of the ingredients in a bowl.

2. SPRINKLE the rub heavily on large cuts of pork and then massage it well into the meat. Allow the seasoned meat to sit for at least 45 minutes at room temperature, or up to overnight wrapped or covered in the refrigerator, prior to cooking.

3. STORE any remaining rub in a covered container in a cool, dark pantry for up to several months.

spicing **TIP** In many of our dry seasonings, we recommend raw turbinado sugar, marketed by one supplier as "Sugar in the Raw." The coarser crystals of this steam-cleaned-by-turbine brown sugar add texture for sure, but they also stay drier on the surface of foods than brown sugar does. Turbinado sugar is extracted from pure sugar cane.

SMOKE AND SPICE

FOR TRADITIONAL BARBECUE

In recent years Cheryl has adopted this perky mixture as her signature dry rub, particularly for pork dishes, and she anointed it after our barbecue book *Smoke & Spice*. The coarse texture of the salt and the turbinado sugar crystals helps the mixture grip to the surface of meat. Absolutely super on pork shoulder, ribs, sausages, and more. MAKES ABOUT 2 CUPS

1 cup smoked kosher salt, coarse sea salt, or flaky salt, such as Maldon

1 cup smoked hot or mild Spanish paprika

2 tablespoons turbinado sugar

1 tablespoon ground cayenne, or to taste

1 teaspoon ground cumin

1. STIR together all of the ingredients in a bowl.

2. SPRINKLE the rub heavily on the pork and then massage it well into the meat. Allow the seasoned meat to sit for at least 45 minutes at room temperature, or up to overnight wrapped or covered in the refrigerator, prior to cooking.

3. STORE any remaining rub in a covered container in a cool, dark pantry for up to several months.

spicing **TIP** Instead of relying on commercial smoked salt, we often make our own version of it and other pantry ingredients, usually when we have the smoker fired up for something bigger. Pour coarse or flaky salt, coarse-ground black pepper, or some other spice into a shallow pan in a layer no thicker than 1/2 inch. Smoke for 20 to 30 minutes. Check the smokiness by sprinkling some of the salt on a piece of bread or a cracker and tasting. Return to the smoker for a few more minutes if you want a deeper smoke flavor.

ALIÑO

A spice mixture used in several South American countries, aliño is something of a cross between a dry rub and a paste. It can be rubbed on a fresh pork picnic or butt, both of which are cut from the shoulder, or perhaps some nice double-thick chops. You might consider it, multiplied several times, on whole hog barbecue as well. To prepare the aliño, first put together the blend of dried spices at your leisure. You can do this well in advance of using the mixture. When you're ready to cook, blend the dry mix with the vinegar, oil, and fresh garlic. The portion given here is plenty for a big pig project, but you can also prepare a smaller amount, enough for a family dinner. Typically, meat marinates in the aliño overnight, so plan accordingly. **MAKES ABOUT 1½ CUPS**

DRY SPICE MIXTURE
1/4 cup kosher salt or coarse sea salt

2 tablespoons achiote paste (see Spicing Tip)

1 tablespoon freshly ground black pepper

2 teaspoons ground cumin

1 teaspoon ground allspice

1 teaspoon ground cinnamon

1/2 teaspoon ground nutmeg

1/2 teaspoon ground cloves

1/2 cup white wine vinegar

1/4 cup extra-virgin olive oil

6 plump garlic cloves

1. STIR together the dry spice mixture in a bowl. Store in a covered container in a cool, dark pantry for up to several months.

2. **WHEN YOU** are ready to make the aliño, dump the dry spices into a blender, add the vinegar, oil, and garlic, and puree. If you want to make a half-size batch of aliño, use just half of the vinegar, oil, and garlic, and save the remaining spice mixture for a second batch at a later time. Rub it generously onto cuts of pork and refrigerate the meat wrapped or covered overnight prior to cooking.

spicing **TIP** **Rusty red achiote paste is a blend of crushed annatto seeds, garlic, vinegar, and other seasonings, often the ones included in the dry spice mixture used in the recipes for Aliño and for Yucatan Rojito. It typically comes in paper- or cardboard-wrapped rectangular bricks of several ounces. Look for it wherever Mexican or Latin American spices are sold. The color comes from the annatto seeds.**

FENNEL SEASONING SALT

Do you like those little starbursts of warm anise-like zest in Italian sausage? If so, this blend is for you, for rubbing over a pork roast or some chops, or perhaps coating sausage patties. MAKES ABOUT ³/₄ CUP

> 1/4 cup fennel seeds
> 1/4 cup kosher salt or coarse sea salt
> 2 tablespoons granulated garlic
> 2 tablespoons dried red bell pepper flakes
> 1 tablespoon crumbled dried marjoram
> 1 teaspoon ground cinnamon

1. **CRUSH** the fennel seeds coarsely in a mortar or with a spice grinder. Dump them out into a small bowl. Stir in the remaining ingredients.

2. **SPRINKLE** the rub heavily on pork and then massage it in well. Allow the seasoned meat to sit for at least 30 minutes at room temperature, or up to overnight wrapped or covered in the refrigerator, prior to cooking.

3. **STORE** any remaining salt in a covered container in a cool, dark pantry for up to several months.

TACOS AL PASTOR PASTE

FOR GRILLED DISHES

The pork for tacos al pastor sizzles on a vertical spit in the same way as for lamb gyros or doner kebabs. Middle Eastern immigration to Mexico probably provided the inspiration for this pork preparation many years ago. As the outer layer of meat is cooked by the fire, it is shaved off for the taco filling. For home cooking, most people use a horizontal spit to hold and rotate a pork shoulder or roast, and they spritz the meat with pineapple juice while it cooks. One of the keys to abundant flavor in the meat is to tuck the seasoning paste into every nook. To provide a double dose of flavor, this recipe makes enough to rub the pork with a portion of the paste before cooking and then again during the cooking. **MAKES ABOUT 1³/₄ CUPS**

> 1 cup pineapple juice
> ¹/₂ medium onion
> 3 or 4 garlic cloves
> 2 or 3 canned chipotle chiles in adobo, plus 2 tablespoons adobo sauce from the can
> 2 tablespoons vegetable oil or sunflower oil
> 2 teaspoons kosher salt or coarse sea salt

1. PUREE all of the ingredients in a blender. Divide the paste into two equal portions. Rub half onto the pork right away. Allow the seasoned meat to sit for at least 45 minutes at room temperature, or up to overnight wrapped or covered in the refrigerator, prior to cooking.

2. ABOUT HALFWAY through the cooking time, rub the meat with the reserved portion of the paste, preferably using a pair of washable barbecue mitts.

FENWAY PARK MUSTARD PASTE

FOR CONTEMPORARY SMOKED FOOD & GRILLED DISHES

Mustard rules when it comes to making seasoning pastes. It has just the right "cling." We often opt for Dijon mustard when we're working with poultry, but for pork, common yellow ballpark-style mustard adds a delectable tang. This paste is so undemanding to assemble that we just make up the amount we need for any batch of pork chops, sausages, or maybe even some franks. If you plan to slather pre-made sausages or dogs, use the smaller amount of salt. MAKES ABOUT ⅓ CUP

> 1/4 cup yellow mustard
> 1 tablespoon vegetable oil or sunflower oil
> 1 teaspoon onion powder
> 1/2 to 1 teaspoon kosher salt or coarse sea salt

1. MIX all of the ingredients in a small bowl.

2. RUB the mixture heavily on small cuts of pork and then massage it well into the meat. Allow the seasoned meat to sit for at least 15 minutes at room temperature, or up to a few hours wrapped or covered in the refrigerator, prior to cooking.

HESTIA'S FIERY RED CHILE PASTE

FOR TRADITIONAL BARBECUE, CONTEMPORARY SMOKED FOOD, & GRILLED DISHES

We fancy that Hestia, the Greek goddess of the hearth and the overseer of cooking, would love this fiery blend of coarsely ground dried red chile. New Mexicans know this elemental mixture as chile caribe. If you're using the paste for grilling, be sure to keep the fire's temperature in the medium heat range. **MAKES ABOUT 3 CUPS**

> 8 ounces (20 to 25) dried whole New Mexican red chile pods—mild, medium, hot, or a combination
>
> 1 teaspoon kosher salt or coarse sea salt, or to taste

1. TOAST the chiles, in several batches, in a cast-iron skillet over medium heat. Remove the chiles from the skillet as soon as they are fragrant.

2. WHEN THE chiles are cool enough to handle, break off the stems and discard the seeds from the pods (wear rubber or plastic gloves if your skin is sensitive). Transfer the chiles to a medium-size saucepan and cover with at least 2 cups water. Bring the water to a quick boil and remove from the heat. Let the chiles soak in the water until soft, about 20 minutes. Taste the soaking water. If bitter, drain off and discard. If not, reserve 2 cups of the liquid.

3. TRANSFER the chiles to a blender. Pour in the reserved 2 cups soaking water (or 2 cups fresh water) and puree.

4. IF YOU wish, scrape the chile paste into a strainer and push the mixture through, discarding the bits of skin left behind. Otherwise, the paste is ready to use or can be transferred to a covered container and refrigerated for up to a month. Rub the mixture heavily on large cuts of pork and then massage it well into the meat. Allow the seasoned meat to sit for at least 45 minutes at room temperature, or up to overnight wrapped or covered in the refrigerator, prior to cooking.

spicing **TIP** It's pretty darned easy to simply pick up a bottled spice or spice blend from a mega-corporation at a chain supermarket and call it good. A more thorough search can reap big rewards in flavor. Towns of all sizes these days have dedicated spice stores where small quantities of spices are ground regularly for maximum freshness. And others are just a click or three away on the Internet. We've long admired the Milwaukee-based Spice House (thespicehouse.com), now more than five decades old, with locations in the upper Midwest, and another Wisconsin-based family company, Penzeys (penzeys.com), that has expanded to cities across the country. A newer small collection of stores is Savory Spice Shop (savoryspiceshop.com), based in Boulder, with a growing number of stores, including one in our hometown of Santa Fe.

YUCATAN ROJITO

When people see a rub, paste, or marinade with brick-red achiote, it's often incorrectly assumed that the seasoning is laced with red chile. In this blend, however, there really is some of the hot stuff. While Aliño (page 14) has South American roots, this one is Mexican in essence. If you are using it for grilling, like on a pork tenderloin, be sure to keep the fire's temperature in the medium heat range. We use this more commonly for something bigger, such as a slower-and-lower-cooked pork shoulder, especially one prepared in Yucatan's signature banana-leaf wrapped style, known as *cochinita pibil*. Pair the meat with a fruity sauce at the table, such as Grilled Pineapple, Chile, and Almond Pico de Gallo (page 55). MAKES ABOUT 1 CUP

> 3.5-ounce package achiote paste (see Spicing Tip, page 15)
>
> 2 tablespoons ground dried pasilla or ancho chile
>
> 1 tablespoon freshly grated orange zest
>
> 2 teaspoons granulated garlic or 1½ teaspoons garlic powder
>
> 2 teaspoons ground mace or 1 teaspoon ground nutmeg
>
> 2 teaspoons kosher salt or coarse sea salt

1. COMBINE all of the ingredients in a food processor until evenly blended. Use immediately or transfer to a covered container and refrigerate for up to several weeks.

2. RUB the mixture heavily on pork cuts and then massage it well into the meat. Allow the seasoned meat to sit for at least 45 minutes at room temperature, or up to overnight wrapped or covered in the refrigerator, prior to cooking.

BACON-ROSEMARY PASTE

Oh, mercy. Smear this into and all around pork butt or picnic, or onto pork chops or baby back ribs, and you're living high on the hog. You can make the paste in a double or triple quantity if you happen to have large quantities of bacon fat at your disposal. MAKES ABOUT 1/3 CUP

1/4 cup bacon drippings
1 garlic clove, minced
1 tablespoon dried rosemary
1 teaspoon Dijon mustard
1 teaspoon kosher salt or coarse sea salt

1. MELT the bacon drippings in a small skillet over medium heat. Stir in the garlic and cook for 1 minute. Stir in the rosemary, mustard, and salt and remove from the heat. Let sit until cool and beginning to firm.

2. USE right away or transfer to a covered container and refrigerate for up to a couple of weeks. Rub the mixture heavily on large cuts of pork and then massage it in well. Allow the seasoned meat to sit for at least 45 minutes at room temperature, or up to overnight wrapped or covered in the refrigerator, prior to cooking.

FRESH HORSERADISH AND MAPLE PASTE

Fresh horseradish root is a great fixing to keep stashed in your refrigerator's crisper drawer. It will retain its potency for weeks and, like a hunk of good Parmesan, can be grated and showered over all kinds of meats to give a final boost of flavor. This paste is best made up as you want to use it, on a ham or other large piece of pork. The mixture can easily be doubled if you need more. MAKES ABOUT 1/2 CUP

> 1/4 cup freshly grated horseradish
> 2 tablespoons pure maple syrup
> 1 tablespoon Dijon mustard
> 1 teaspoon kosher salt or coarse salt

1. **STIR** together all of the ingredients in a small bowl.

2. **USE** the paste right away, by massaging it heavily on pork. Allow the seasoned meat to sit for at least 45 minutes at room temperature, or up to overnight wrapped or covered in the refrigerator, prior to cooking.

SRIRACHA, SOY, AND SESAME MARINADE

We're tampering here with the Chinese-style barbecued pork flavoring called char siu, which mixes sweet and savory flavors along with a healthy shot of red food coloring. We've cut the food coloring, added a few squirts of tangy hot sriracha, and then balanced the sweetness with the toasty flavor of sesame oil. This is great on lightly smoked foods, but the sesame would get lost on long-smoked barbecue. **MAKES ABOUT 2 CUPS**

1 cup soy sauce

1/2 cup pineapple juice or syrup from a can of lychees

1/4 cup ketchup

2 tablespoons Asian sesame oil

2 teaspoons hoisin sauce

2 teaspoons sriracha, or more to taste

1 or 2 crushed star anise or 1 teaspoon five-spice powder

1. WHISK together all of the ingredients in a bowl or combine them in a large zipper-lock plastic bag.

2. USE the marinade right away or cover and refrigerate it for up to a couple of days. Pour the marinade over the pork and let sit for at least 30 minutes at room temperature, or refrigerate wrapped or covered up to overnight, prior to cooking.

HONEY-SAGE MARINADE

FOR TRADITIONAL BARBECUE, CONTEMPORARY SMOKED FOOD, & GRILLED DISHES

Here's a case where dried herbs will bolster the flavor of the marinade more fully than fresh. Save fresh sage for Fried Sage Leaves (page 65) or use it as a special garnish for your dish. MAKES ABOUT 1³/₄ CUPS

> 1 cup apple juice or cider
> ¹/₂ cup honey
> 2 tablespoons extra-virgin olive oil
> 1 tablespoon crumbled dried sage
> 2 garlic cloves, minced
> 1 teaspoon kosher salt or coarse sea salt
> 1 teaspoon freshly ground black pepper

1. WHISK together all of the ingredients in a bowl or combine them in a large zipper-lock plastic bag.

2. USE the marinade right away or refrigerate it in a covered container for up to a couple of days. Pour the marinade over the pork and let sit for at least 30 minutes at room temperature, or refrigerate wrapped or covered up to overnight, prior to cooking.

> **VARIATION:** If sage isn't a favorite of yours, leave it out and add a chopped shallot and then a tablespoon or so of crumbled dried thyme or rosemary.

RUM AND MANGO MARINADE

FOR TRADITIONAL BARBECUE, CONTEMPORARY SMOKED FOOD, & GRILLED DISHES

It takes two to tango, of course, and the same for samba. This marinade will have most pork cuts stepping lively, particularly a grilled pork tenderloin or smoky spare ribs. The sugars in the fruit nectar and rum will caramelize sassily on the surface of the meat. Quick Mango Chutney–Pickapeppa Glaze (page 49) will boost the pizzazz at the table. MAKES ABOUT 2 CUPS

3/4 cup light rum

1/4 cup dark rum

1 cup mango nectar

1 tablespoon vegetable oil or sunflower oil

1 tablespoon white vinegar

1 teaspoon kosher salt or coarse sea salt

A few splashes of Caribbean hot sauce

1. **WHISK** together all of the ingredients in a bowl or a large zipper-lock plastic bag.

2. **USE** the marinade within a few hours for the best flavor. Cover the pork in the marinade and let it sit for at least 30 minutes at room temperature, or refrigerate wrapped or covered up to overnight, prior to cooking.

MOPS AND BASTES

WORCESTERSHIRE MOP

FOR TRADITIONAL BARBECUE & CONTEMPORARY SMOKED FOOD

We love this mop on Memphis ribs, the "dry" kind that are coated all crusty in a rub and served without sauce. Mopping or drizzling that style of ribs with some of this scrumptious mixture keeps the meat extra-succulent while building up another layer of flavor. It's a fine mop for other pork, too. If you are working with a lean cut like tenderloin, stir an additional tablespoon of vegetable oil or lard into the mop. **MAKES ABOUT 3¼ CUPS**

2 cups cider vinegar

¹/₂ cup water

¹/₄ cup Worcestershire sauce

¹/₄ cup packed dark brown sugar

2 tablespoons vegetable or sunflower oil, lard, or bacon drippings

1 tablespoon kosher salt or coarse sea salt

2 teaspoons Tabasco sauce or other vinegar-based hot sauce

1. COMBINE all of the ingredients in a saucepan.

2. HEAT the mop before you plan to use it initially, and keep it warm over low heat between bastes. Apply to large cuts of meat about once an hour and smaller cuts twice per hour.

TIME-TESTED BEER AND VINEGAR MOP

FOR TRADITIONAL BARBECUE

Beer and vinegar rank as the most popular liquids for mopping authentic barbecue. This blend of the two contributes a contrasting tang to the richness of pork, especially a cut like shoulder or even a whole hog. When cooked, the crusty pork, encased in dark "bark," melds with virtually any of our classic barbecue sauces coming up later in the chapter. Our first choice would be Pig Pickin' Vinegar Sauce (page 35). **MAKES ABOUT 4 CUPS**

12-ounce bottle or can decent-quality beer

1 cup cider vinegar or white vinegar

1 cup water

1/4 cup vegetable or sunflower oil

1/2 medium onion, chopped or sliced in thin half-moons

2 tablespoons kosher salt or coarse sea salt

2 tablespoons freshly ground black pepper

1. COMBINE all of the ingredients in a saucepan.

2. HEAT the mop before you plan to use it initially and keep it warm over low heat between bastes. Apply to the meat about once an hour.

VARIATION: Use one of today's popular Belgian beers and, to complement its citrusy undertones, replace the vinegar with orange juice. Add a few slices of fresh orange, too, if you wish.

spicing **TIP** Because a mop keeps bubbling over a fire during long periods of smoking, some of it will evaporate. You can stir some hot water back into it, but don't do that so much that the flavor evaporates, too. Simply make yourself another batch, or just doctor what you have with a little more beer, vinegar, or other tasty liquid.

SWEET COFFEE SOP

This mop pairs especially well with spare ribs or pork butt massaged with Sweet Brunette Rub (page 8) and finished at the table with Sweet Coffee-Cascabel Sauce (page 39). MAKES ABOUT 3$^1/_2$ CUPS

2 cups brewed coffee

$^1/_2$ cup apple cider or juice

$^1/_2$ cup ketchup

$^1/_2$ cup Worcestershire sauce

2 tablespoons unsalted butter

1 tablespoon packed dark brown sugar

1. COMBINE all of the ingredients in a saucepan.

2. HEAT the mop before you plan to use it initially and keep it warm over low heat between bastes. Apply to large cuts of meat about once an hour and smaller cuts twice per hour.

BUTTERY CABERNET BASTE

One of those remarkable French emulsions, beurre rouge, inspired this baste. In an emulsion, fat becomes suspended in liquid, which of course is not its natural state. That means this baste won't hold forever, so it's not a great candidate for pairing with a seriously barbecued large chunk of pork. It is, however, a sophisticated partner for grilled chops or smoked tenderloin medallions, or when you're simply adding smoke to a precooked ham. Beurre rouge is versatile enough to blanket a beefsteak or even a side of salmon, too, and it can be used to sauce a finished dish. If you want to work with a single pork tenderloin, or just a couple of chops, you can halve the recipe.

MAKES ABOUT 1¼ CUPS

1 cup Cabernet Sauvignon or other dry red wine
$1/2$ cup red wine vinegar
$1/4$ cup minced shallots
Pinch of sugar
1 cup (2 sticks) cold unsalted butter, cut in 1-tablespoon pats
Kosher salt or coarse sea salt

1. COMBINE the wine, vinegar, shallots, and sugar in a saucepan. Bring to a boil over medium heat and cook until the liquid is reduced to ¼ cup.

2. REDUCE the heat to low. Whisk the butter into the sauce, 1 piece at a time, until all of it is incorporated. Add salt to taste.

3. BASTE the meat as you start the cooking and when it begins to look dry. Keep the basting liquid over low heat between bastes.

DR P GLAZE

You can't have a bunch of barbecue sauces without Southern soft drinks included in the ingredients. Paint this mixture on ribs or chops while they are smoking, or just before chops or tenderloin come off the grill. You'll also find it amazingly good on smoked halved softball-size sweet onions.

MAKES ABOUT 2 CUPS

12-ounce bottle or can Dr Pepper

1/4 cup A.1. Original steak sauce

1 tablespoon Dijon mustard

1 tablespoon corn syrup

1 tablespoon unsalted butter

1/2 teaspoon freshly ground black pepper

1. COMBINE all of the ingredients in a large saucepan and warm the glaze over medium heat. Cook for about 10 minutes, just enough for the flavors to meld.

2. BASTE the pork with a portion of the glaze near the end of the cooking time. Stored in a covered container, the glaze will keep in the refrigerator for at least a month.

VARIATIONS: Trade out the Dr Pepper for root beer, cream soda, Cherry Coke, or RC Cola.

SAUCES

PIG PICKIN' VINEGAR SAUCE

FOR TRADITIONAL BARBECUE & CONTEMPORARY SMOKED FOOD

A thin, puckery sauce of this style opened Cheryl's eyes to the wonders of barbecue decades ago while she was traveling south on a family vacation in the Chevy station wagon. Few things so eye-opening are simpler to whip together. This vinegar slather complements any kind of smoked pig, whether it be a whole hog, shoulder, or even a passel of country-style pork chops.

MAKES ABOUT 2^1/$_2$ CUPS

2 cups cider vinegar or white vinegar

$1/2$ cup water

2 tablespoons light brown sugar or granulated sugar

1 tablespoon kosher salt or coarse sea salt, or more to taste

2 teaspoons coarsely ground black pepper

1 teaspoon ground cayenne or crushed hot red chile flakes

1. STIR together all of the ingredients in a medium-size bowl until the sugar dissolves. Alternatively, shake everything together in a covered quart-size canning jar.

2. SERVE the sauce at room temperature or chill, covered, for later use. It keeps almost indefinitely in a covered container in the refrigerator. If serving the sauce with pulled pork, mix enough of the sauce into the meat to make it moist before serving with additional sauce on the side.

DOUBLE MUSTARD SAUCE, SOUTHERN STYLE

This sauce is modeled on ones common in South Carolina and Georgia, but tinkered with to our own taste. You won't find a tomato anywhere here.

MAKES ABOUT 2 CUPS

> 3/4 cup white vinegar
> 1/2 cup yellow mustard
> 1/2 cup coarse-grain brown mustard
> 1/3 cup water
> 1 medium onion, minced
> 1 tablespoon packed brown sugar
> 1 teaspoon celery seeds
> 1/2 teaspoon freshly ground black pepper
> 1/2 teaspoon kosher salt or coarse sea salt

1. COMBINE all of the ingredients in a saucepan and bring to a simmer over medium-high heat. Reduce the heat to low and cook until the onion is tender and the sauce thickens, 20 to 25 minutes.

2. SERVE the sauce warm or chilled on or alongside smoked pork. Stored in a covered container, the sauce will keep in the refrigerator for about 2 weeks.

SWEET AND SOUR HONEY-MUSTARD BARBECUE SAUCE

Inspiration for this sauce comes from the Salt Lick, a barbecue bastion just outside Austin. The sauce actually strikes us as too sweet for Texas brisket and other beef, but we think it pairs perfectly with pork. The sauce's flavor reminds us of the poppy seed dressing that has topped many a salad in Texas over the years. If you don't want to bother grating an onion on the side of your cheese grater, you can substitute onion powder. In this case, however, we prefer the real thing. MAKES ABOUT 2 CUPS

1/2 cup cider vinegar

1/2 cup mild-flavored honey

2 teaspoons dried mustard powder

2 teaspoons grated onion

2 teaspoons Worcestershire sauce

1 teaspoon sweet paprika

1 teaspoon freshly ground black pepper

1/2 teaspoon garlic powder

1/2 teaspoon ground dried ginger

1/2 teaspoon kosher salt or coarse sea salt

Pinch of ground cloves

1 cup vegetable oil or sunflower oil

1. COMBINE in a food processor or blender the vinegar, honey, dry mustard, onion, Worcestershire sauce, paprika, black pepper, garlic powder, ginger, salt, and cloves and process until well blended. With the processor running, drizzle in the oil in a slow, steady stream until all of it is incorporated.

2. THE SAUCE can be used at room temperature or warmed over low heat to serve on or alongside cuts of pork. Stored in a covered container, it will keep in the refrigerator for several weeks.

CHARRED HABANERO-PEACH BARBECUE SAUCE

This sauce is spicy but not off the charts. Incendiary habaneros are known for their floral, fruity flavor, if you can keep the heat under control, as we do here. The fruitiness of the chile mates well with lush fruits like summer peaches. MAKES ABOUT 2 CUPS

> 1 fresh habanero or Scotch bonnet chile
> 1/2 medium onion
> 1 pound peaches, peeled, pitted, and chopped
> 1/4 cup water
> 3 tablespoons brown sugar
> 1/2 teaspoon Worcestershire sauce
> 1/2 teaspoon cider vinegar or other fruit vinegar
> 1/4 teaspoon ground cumin
> 1/2 teaspoon kosher salt or coarse sea salt, or more to taste

1. WARM a small cast-iron skillet over high heat. Place in it the habanero and onion. Turn each with tongs until somewhat charred on all sides, 5 to 10 minutes. Do not stand directly over the chile while its potent fumes are released. The onion will soften somewhat, but your goal is just to get the char on all surfaces. Remove from the heat and set aside to cool.

2. WHEN COOL enough to handle, don rubber gloves and cut out the chile's stem and seeds and discard them. Chunk the onion half into several pieces.

3. TRANSFER the habanero, onion, peaches, and water to a food processor. (This can be done in batches if necessary.) Puree the mixture, then pour it into a saucepan. Add the remaining ingredients and bring to a simmer. Reduce the heat to low and cook until thickened and sauce-like, 25 to 30 minutes.

4. SERVE the sauce warm or at room temperature on or alongside cuts of pork. Stored in a covered container in the refrigerator, it will keep for several weeks.

VARIATION: If it's not fresh peach season, substitute mango or even papaya. With papaya, you may need to put in an extra 1/4 cup water to get a good sauce consistency.

SWEET COFFEE-CASCABEL SAUCE

FOR TRADITIONAL BARBECUE, CONTEMPORARY SMOKED FOOD, & GRILLED DISHES

Cascabel is a small, round, fruity dried chile that blends well with this sauce's sweet tones. You can substitute ground New Mexican red chile, though, if it's easier to find. MAKES ABOUT 2 CUPS

> 1 tablespoon vegetable or sunflower oil
> 1/2 medium onion, minced
> 2 cups brewed coffee
> 1/4 cup light brown sugar or turbinado sugar
> 1 tablespoon corn syrup
> 1 to 2 teaspoons ground dried cascabel chile
> 1/2 teaspoon ground cinnamon
> Kosher salt or coarse sea salt
> 1 tablespoon unsalted butter

1. WARM the oil in a small saucepan over medium heat. Stir in the onion and cook until it begins to soften, about 5 minutes.

2. ADD the coffee, brown sugar, corn syrup, chile, cinnamon, and salt to taste. Simmer until the mixture is reduced by about one-third, about 10 minutes. Whisk in the butter. Serve the sauce warm with dinner. You can also store it in a covered container in the refrigerator for several weeks, but reheat it before using.

RYE WHISKEY AND MAPLE BARBECUE SAUCE

We used to whip up a sauce similar to this with bourbon. However, with the wide availability of rye as a spirit, we've switched over in recent years. We prefer the spicier, fruitier taste of the rye to the smoother, sweeter bourbon profile. The sauce is such a personal favorite that you might find us drinking it and forgetting all about the hog. **MAKES ABOUT 3 CUPS**

4 tablespoons (1/2 stick) unsalted butter

1/4 cup vegetable or sunflower oil

2 cups minced onion

3/4 cup rye whiskey

3/4 cup pure maple syrup

2/3 cup ketchup

1/2 cup orange juice

1/2 cup cider vinegar or white vinegar

2 tablespoons Worcestershire sauce

1/2 teaspoon kosher salt or coarse sea salt, or more to taste

1/2 teaspoon freshly ground black pepper

1. COMBINE the butter and oil in a medium-size saucepan over medium heat. When the butter melts, add the onion and sauté until golden, about 7 minutes.

2. MIX in the remaining ingredients, reduce the heat to low, and cook the mixture until thickened and reduced, about 30 minutes. Stir frequently during the last 10 minutes of the cooking time.

3. SERVE the sauce warm or at room temperature on or alongside cuts of pork. Stored in a covered container in the refrigerator, the sauce will keep for several weeks, but warm it before serving again.

GINGER-TANGERINE FINISHING SAUCE

Zingy and zesty, the heat of the ginger hits you right up front, and white pepper reinforces the blast on the back end without calling attention to itself. Sure, you can substitute orange juice for tangerine if you need to, but there's an extra-special freshness to tangerine or clementine juice when they are available in the winter months. MAKES ABOUT 1½ CUPS

1 tablespoon vegetable or sunflower oil

Walnut-size chunk of fresh ginger, minced

1 cup orange marmalade

½ teaspoon finely ground white pepper

½ cup fresh tangerine or clementine juice, from 2 or 3 tangerines or 4 or 5 clementines

1. WARM the oil in a small saucepan over medium heat. Stir in the ginger and cook until softened, about 5 minutes. Stir in the orange marmalade and pepper and cook until the marmalade has melted into a thick sauce. Remove from the heat and stir in the tangerine juice. If the marmalade is especially chunky, cool the sauce briefly, then puree it in a food processer or blender.

2. BASTE the pork with a portion of the sauce near the end of the cooking time and serve the remaining sauce warm or at room temperature with the food. The sauce can be stored in a covered container in the refrigerator for up to a week, but warm it before serving again.

CENTRAL CAROLINA RED

Much has been made over the gradations of sauces in North Carolina. Near the eastern seaboard, the favored sauce is similar to the previous recipe, Pig Pickin' Vinegar Sauce, but by the time one gets to the western border, the sauce has been tinted heavily with tomatoes, as in the variation below. We plop down right in the middle of the state with this version, a mixture that claims most of the hearts and minds in the central region. All the Carolina sauces tend to be on the thin side, because they are typically tossed with pulled or chopped bits of pork and coat the meat most easily this way.

MAKES ABOUT 2 CUPS

1 1/2 cups cider vinegar

1/2 cup ketchup

1 tablespoon granulated sugar

1 1/2 teaspoons kosher salt or coarse sea salt

1/2 teaspoon ground cayenne or crushed hot red chile flakes

1/2 teaspoon ground white pepper

1. STIR together all of the ingredients in a medium-size bowl until the sugar dissolves. Alternatively, shake everything together in a covered quart-size canning jar.

2. SERVE the sauce at room temperature or chill, covered, for later use. It keeps almost indefinitely in a covered container in the refrigerator. If you're serving the sauce with pulled pork, mix enough of the sauce into the meat to make it moist before serving with additional sauce on the side.

VARIATION: For Western Carolina Sweet and Sour Sauce, reverse the proportions of vinegar and ketchup and leave out the white pepper.

K.C. CLASSIC BBQ SAUCE

When it comes to sauce, Kansas City is the nexus of tomatoes, sugar, and spice. We've whipped up a variety of K.C.-style brews over the years, but this is now our favorite of them all. MAKES ABOUT 2 CUPS

1 tablespoon unsalted butter

1 cup minced onion

2 garlic cloves, minced

8-ounce can tomato sauce

3/4 cup cider vinegar

1/4 cup plus 2 tablespoons packed dark brown sugar

1/4 cup tomato paste

1/4 cup warm water

3 tablespoons Worcestershire sauce

3 tablespoons chili powder

1 tablespoon yellow mustard

1 tablespoon corn syrup

2 teaspoons smoked salt (see Spicing Tip, page 12) or celery salt, or more to taste

2 teaspoons freshly ground black pepper

1. WARM the butter in a saucepan over medium heat. Stir in the onion and garlic and sauté until softened and translucent, about 5 minutes.

2. MIX in the rest of the ingredients and bring the sauce to a simmer. Reduce the heat to low and let it cook until the flavors have blended and the sauce has reduced by about one-third, 25 to 30 minutes. Stir frequently in the last few minutes to avoid scorching. If the sauce is too thick to spoon easily, add a bit more water.

3. SERVE the sauce warm or at room temperature on or alongside the food. Stored in a covered container in the refrigerator, it will keep for several weeks, but warm it before serving again.

WATERMELON-JALAPEÑO SYRUP

FOR TRADITIONAL BARBECUE, CONTEMPORARY SMOKED FOOD, & GRILLED DISHES

What a scrumptious and slightly unexpected combination of sweet summer heat. Slather it on racks of spare ribs or baby backs, a tenderloin or two, or some chops. It's uncomplicated to make your own watermelon juice if you don't have an easy source for it. Simply puree chunks of the melon in your blender. **MAKES ABOUT 1½ CUPS**

> 1 cup fresh watermelon juice
> ½ cup water
> 3 tablespoons granulated sugar
> 2 or 3 fresh jalapeños, seeded and chopped
> 1 garlic clove, minced
> Juice of 1 medium lime

1. COMBINE the watermelon juice, water, sugar, jalapeños, and garlic in a small saucepan. Bring the mixture to a simmer over medium heat, stirring to dissolve the sugar. Remove the syrup from the heat and stir in the lime juice.

2. SERVE warm on or alongside pork at the table. The sauce will keep in a covered container in the refrigerator for up to 5 days, but reheat it before using.

ROASTED ONION RANCH DRESSING

FOR TRADITIONAL BARBECUE & CONTEMPORARY SMOKED FOOD

According to people who track such things, ranch dressing has been America's most popular salad dressing since 1992. Actually, the mixture tops a lot of things that can't be described as salad. We think it's darned fine with pulled pork, whether it's in a bun, served up as a taco in a soft corn tortilla, or in a wrap with some actual green stuff. Roasting the onion gives it a boost.

MAKES ABOUT 2$^1\!/_2$ CUPS

1 medium onion, cut into $^1\!/_2$-inch slices

$^1\!/_2$ cup buttermilk

1 cup mayonnaise

$^1\!/_2$ cup sour cream

1 teaspoon Worcestershire sauce

$^1\!/_2$ teaspoon white vinegar

2 tablespoons minced flat-leaf parsley

1 tablespoon minced fresh chives or dill

Kosher salt or coarse sea salt

1. PREHEAT the oven to 400°F. Lay the onion slices on a baking sheet and spritz them lightly on both sides with vegetable oil spray. Bake the onions until they begin to color and soften, then stir and turn to roast evenly, 12 to 15 minutes total. Let the onions cool briefly.

2. PLACE the onion slices and buttermilk in a food processor and puree. Stop the processor and add the mayonnaise, sour cream, Worcestershire sauce, and vinegar. Pulse the mixture until well combined. Stir in the parsley and chives and salt to taste.

3. COVER and store in the refrigerator for at least 30 minutes or up to a week. Drizzle the chilled dressing onto any type of pulled pork sandwich.

BARBECUE VINAIGRETTE

Sometimes conventional barbecue sauces, especially the tomato-based variety, just seem too heavy for a dish. With a pork tenderloin that has been grilled or smoked, we often opt to mix the hearty sauce with a lighter salad dressing, and *voilà*: barbecue vinaigrette. The tanginess in the mixture lets it work equally well with smoked and grilled fare. **MAKES ABOUT 1¼ CUPS**

3 tablespoons tomato-based barbecue sauce (preferably not super-sweet or super-smoky)

½ cup orange juice

2 teaspoons Worcestershire sauce

1 garlic clove, minced

½ cup vegetable oil or sunflower oil

Kosher salt or coarse sea salt

Freshly ground black pepper

1. WHISK together the barbecue sauce, orange juice, Worcestershire sauce, and garlic in a bowl. Whisk in the oil and season with salt and pepper to taste.

2. SERVE the sauce at the table at room temperature. The sauce will keep in a covered container in the refrigerator for several weeks, but reheat it gently before using again.

VARIATION: For a Citrus Vinaigrette, eliminate the barbecue sauce from the recipe and add 3 extra tablespoons orange juice. Use with similar meats.

POMEGRANATE CREAM SAUCE

FOR GRILLED DISHES

When Cheryl spent time in Mallorca as a twenty-something, she was fascinated by the striking ruby drink sent over by a prospective suitor. She was much more taken by what turned out to be a pomegranate beverage than with the admirer. She's always remembered the experience, though, because it was her first taste of the then hard-to-find and exotic fruit. We have subsequently discovered that all manner of pomegranate concoctions turn out to have Mallorcan roots, including this type of colorful sauce. It's a fine accompaniment to pork, perhaps spooned over slices of a rotisserie-grilled loin or simply grilled tenderloin or chops. **MAKES ABOUT 2 CUPS**

> 2 tablespoons extra-virgin olive oil
>
> 2 tablespoons lard or more extra-virgin olive oil
>
> 1 large onion, finely chopped
>
> 1/2 cup dry white wine
>
> 1 1/2 cups pomegranate juice
>
> 1 cup heavy cream
>
> Seeds of 1 pomegranate
>
> 3/4 teaspoon kosher salt or coarse sea salt, or more to taste
>
> 1/2 teaspoon freshly ground black pepper

1. **WARM** the oil and lard together in a skillet over medium heat. Stir in the onion and cook until soft and translucent, about 7 minutes. Pour in the wine, some of which will evaporate nearly immediately. Pour in the pomegranate juice and the cream and continue cooking until the sauce is reduced by about half, about 15 minutes.

2. **ADD** the pomegranate seeds and the salt and pepper and cook for 5 more minutes. Serve the sauce warm with dinner. It can be refrigerated in a covered container for up to a week, but reheat it before using.

QUICK MANGO CHUTNEY-PICKAPEPPA GLAZE

FOR TRADITIONAL BARBECUE, CONTEMPORARY SMOKED FOOD, & GRILLED DISHES

A couple of our favorite flavors in the world are mango and Jamaican Pickapeppa, a scrumptious condiment somewhat like a sweet, spicier Worcestershire sauce. Imagine our surprise when we looked for more information about both online and discovered that there is actually a Pickapeppa Mango Chutney. So start with it, if you like, and that will make the recipe superswift. We can't get enough of this glaze brushed on pork tenderloin or baby back ribs while they are grilling or smoking or served as a sauce when the meat is done. For a different pairing, use it to glaze jerk chicken in its final few minutes of cooking. **MAKES ABOUT 1½ CUPS**

1 cup mango chutney, any large chunks of mango chopped
6 tablespoons Pickapeppa sauce
2 to 4 tablespoons hot water

1. WHISK together the chutney and Pickapeppa sauce in a bowl. Add enough hot water to make an easily spoonable sauce.

2. USE a portion of the mixture as a baste in the last few minutes of cooking and save the rest of it for a table sauce. It can be refrigerated in a covered container for up to several weeks, but warm it before serving again.

spicing **TIP** You should have a good silicone basting brush among your outdoor cooking tools. Other key equipment is more basic than the manufacturers of doodads would like you to think. Get a good set of tongs with rubber inserts down the sides to keep your hand cool, a sturdy offset-handled spatula, a high-quality digital thermometer, a set of flat metal skewers, a washable barbecue mitt, and a pair of neoprene grilling gloves that can take really high heat.

BACON AND SAGE CREAM

FOR GRILLED DISHES

It's bacon and cream—how could it not be over-the-top good? Serve over any style of grilled tenderloin or pork chops. For a really special occasion, however, turn the sauce into a kingly crown atop hefty porterhouse pork chops or a "tomahawk rack" of chops from Heritage Foods USA (heritagefoodsusa.com). **MAKES ABOUT 1 CUP**

> 3 thick bacon slices, chopped
> 1 garlic clove, minced
> 1 teaspoon white vinegar
> 2 cups heavy cream
> 3 tablespoons chopped fresh sage
> Kosher salt or coarse sea salt

1. COOK the bacon in a saucepan over medium heat. When it is brown and crisp, remove it with a slotted spoon. Stir in the garlic and cook for 1 minute. Pour in the vinegar and let it evaporate. Add the cream and the sage, bring the mixture slowly to a boil, and reduce the sauce by half, about 5 to 10 minutes more.

2. STRAIN the sauce, and stir the bacon back into it. Taste and add salt as you wish. Serve the warm sauce on or alongside premier pork cuts.

SAUCE CHARCUTIÈRE

Here's an old French masterpiece, updated just a touch, making a tangy delight over smoked or grilled pork tenderloin. The sauce comes together quickly, so we make it fresh each time we plan to use it. MAKES ABOUT 1¼ CUPS

> 1 tablespoon lard or unsalted butter
> 3 tablespoons minced onion
> 8 ounces demi-glace
> 1 teaspoon Dijon mustard
> 2 tablespoons minced cornichon pickles
> Kosher salt or coarse sea salt

1. WARM the lard in a sauté pan over medium heat. Stir in the onion and cook until soft and translucent, about 7 minutes. Stir in the demi-glace and mustard until combined and heated through.

2. REMOVE the sauce from the heat and whisk in the pickles. Taste and add salt as needed. Serve warm at the table.

spicing **TIP** **This sauce uses demi-glace, a greatly reduced rich stock, as the liquid. You can purchase decent-quality demi-glace at supermarkets and online; one widely available brand is Demi-Glace Gold.**

JEZEBEL SAUCE

Like pimiento cheese, Jezebel sauce, another traditional Southern condiment, is more than the sum of its parts. The name likely refers to the biblical temptress since the sauce has a wicked kick an eater might not see coming. While there's nothing finer on a smoked ham, this is also killer good on grilled pork chops or tenderloin. Oh, and save some to serve over a chunk of cream cheese or fresh goat cheese, with crackers. **MAKES ABOUT 2 CUPS**

1/3 cup prepared horseradish
3 tablespoons dried mustard powder
1 to 2 teaspoons freshly ground black pepper
10-ounce jar "all-fruit" apricot or peach preserves
10-ounce jar apple jelly

1. WHISK together the horseradish, mustard powder, and pepper in a large bowl. Spoon in the preserves and jelly, and whisk until the sauce is well blended and smooth.

2. SERVE the sauce at room temperature or chilled on or alongside cuts of pork. It can be stored in a covered container in the refrigerator for at least a couple of months.

CRAFT BEER BUTTER

No, we didn't whip this up after happy hour at a craft brewery. The idea of adding fresh hops panicles, or shoots, to make a beer butter actually goes back to *Larousse Gastronomique*, the early-twentieth-century French cooking guide. The hops, often sold in farmers' markets these days, give a pleasant bitterness to the butter, as they do to beer itself, and will also be a novelty to most guests. **MAKES ABOUT 1 CUP**

12-ounce bottle or can medium-bodied beer
2 tablespoons fresh hops panicles, optional
1 garlic clove, minced, optional
8 tablespoons (1 stick) unsalted butter, cut into 8 pieces
Kosher salt or coarse sea salt

1. POUR the beer into a saucepan, and add the hops and garlic, if you wish. Over medium heat, reduce the mixture by half.

2. REDUCE the heat to low. Whisk the butter into the sauce, one piece at a time, until all of it is incorporated. Sprinkle in salt to your taste. Serve warm at the table on or alongside grilled pork.

OTHER CONDIMENTS FOR FLAVORING

PICKLED RED ONIONS

FOR TRADITIONAL BARBECUE, CONTEMPORARY SMOKED FOOD, & GRILLED DISHES

Scrumptious served with virtually any pork, these Mexican-inspired onions are a traditional accompaniment to *cochinita pibil* **and other dishes.**

MAKES ABOUT 1½ CUPS

> 1 medium red onion, sliced into very thin rings
> Hot water
> 3/4 cup red wine vinegar
> 1/4 cup water
> 2 tablespoons packed brown sugar
> 1 fresh jalapeño or serrano chile, seeded and thinly sliced, optional
> 1 teaspoon black peppercorns

1. PLACE the onion rings in a medium-size bowl. Pour in enough hot water to cover them by about 1 inch. Let the onion rings stand for 15 minutes, then pour off and discard the water.

2. COMBINE the vinegar, water, brown sugar, chile (if you are using it), and peppercorns in a small saucepan over medium-high heat and bring just to a boil. Pour the liquid over the onion rings and stir to combine. Cover and refrigerate for at least 2 hours.

3. SERVE the pickled onions chilled alongside pork. The onions will keep in a covered container in the refrigerator for at least 2 weeks.

GRILLED PINEAPPLE, CHILE, AND ALMOND PICO DE GALLO

The nuts add a touch of surprise to this fresh relish, along with a welcome crunch. The recipe makes quite a bit simply because of the size of a fresh pineapple. If you wish, you can make just a half batch of pico de gallo and save the other half of the pineapple for dessert or another meal.

MAKES ABOUT 3 CUPS

1 medium fresh pineapple or 1 pound fresh pineapple slices

1/2 cup Marcona almonds, toasted or roasted, salted or unsalted

1/2 cup chopped red onion

1 fresh jalapeño or serrano chile, seeded and minced

2 to 3 tablespoons minced fresh cilantro

1 tablespoon extra-virgin olive oil

Kosher salt or coarse sea salt, optional

1. FIRE up the grill, bringing the temperature to medium (where you can hold your hand an inch or two over the cooking grate for 4 to 5 seconds before you need to pull it away).

2. IF YOU have a whole pineapple, slice off the top. Cut a small slice off the bottom so that it rests evenly. Cut off all of the pineapple skin, slicing as deeply as needed to remove the tiny brown eyes. Cut the pineapple into 1/2-inch-thick slices, discarding all portions of the fibrous core. Spritz the pineapple slices with olive oil spray on both sides.

3. GRILL the pineapple slices, uncovered, until softened, with a few brown and caramelized edges on both sides, about 5 minutes. Let the slices cool, then slice each ring into neat tidbits, like we all used to eat from the can as kids. You should have approximately 2 heaping cups of pineapple.

4. STIR together the pineapple, almonds, onion, chile, cilantro, and olive oil in a large bowl. Taste the pico de gallo and add salt if necessary—you might not need any if you are using salted almonds. Serve right away or store in a covered container in the refrigerator for up to several hours. Use at room temperature or chilled.

CATALAN QUINCE AND GARLIC ALLIOLI

FOR GRILLED DISHES

Have you ever had the traditional combo of quince paste, called membrillo, and Spanish Manchego cheese? That pairing of sweet with savory got us searching for and playing around with other similar ideas. From the center of Catalan cuisine in northeast Spain, around Barcelona, comes this garlicky olive oil condiment, something like a mayonnaise without eggs. Sometimes the spread incorporates fruit, such as quince, that grows in the area. Look for quinces in a well-stocked produce section in the fall, when they will probably sit near the apples and pears that they resemble in appearance and fragrance. Quinces need to be cooked to be palatable, and the cooking time can be a bit unpredictable. They will soften eventually, though. **MAKES ABOUT 1½ CUPS**

1 large quince, peeled, cored, and cut into 1-inch cubes
4 plump garlic cloves, sliced
½ teaspoon kosher salt or coarse sea salt, or more to taste
⅓ to ½ cup extra-virgin olive oil

1. PLACE the quince in a small saucepan and cover with water. Bring to a simmer over medium heat and cook until soft, 15 to 25 minutes. Drain the quince.

2. COMBINE the garlic with ½ teaspoon salt in a mortar and work with the pestle until the garlic has broken down into a paste. Add the quince and use the pestle to mash and combine it. Stir in the oil, a few drops at a time, working it into the paste to form an emulsion. Use only as much oil as you need to achieve an emulsion.

3. SERVE the allioli right away with grilled pork, or refrigerate in a covered container for up to several hours.

SHERRIED APPLE CONSERVA

FOR GRILLED DISHES

Dry sherry complements this Spanish-inspired conserva, something of a high-octane chunky applesauce. We think sherry can taste a bit muddy with smoked foods but find it a fine match for grilled dishes, especially pork. Grilled lamb chops are good topped with the mixture, too. MAKES ABOUT 2 CUPS

> 2 tablespoons olive oil
>
> 2 cups chopped peeled tangy apples, such as Granny Smith or Jonathan
>
> 3/4 cup diced red onion
>
> 2 teaspoons minced garlic
>
> 1 cup dry sherry
>
> 1/4 cup packed light brown sugar
>
> 1/4 teaspoon kosher salt or coarse sea salt, or more to taste

1. WARM the oil in a saucepan over medium heat. Stir in the apples, onion, and garlic and cook until soft, about 10 minutes. Stir every few minutes to make sure the mixture isn't sticking. Apples have differing amounts of moisture, so if the mixture is drying out before softening, add a tablespoon or two of water.

2. ONCE THE mixture is soft, mix in the sherry, brown sugar, and salt. Bring to a simmer, then reduce the heat to low and cook until jammy, about 10 minutes more. Serve warm or at room temperature. The conserva will keep in a covered container in the refrigerator for at least a week, but reheat it before serving.

SAVORY ORANGE CONFIT

Argentina's most famous chef, Francis Mallmann, is known for his astonishing repertoire of grilled foods. We had the pleasure of meeting him and observing his techniques recently. This idea, something like an herb-scented marmalade, comes from the chef, and we like it best on grilled pork chops or tenderloin or a smoked ham. MAKES ABOUT 1½ CUPS

> 4 medium to large oranges, halved through their equators
> 12 black peppercorns
> 3 bay leaves
> 1 cup dry white wine
> 1 teaspoon kosher salt or coarse sea salt, or more to taste
> About 1 cup olive oil

1. SQUEEZE the juice from the oranges into a large saucepan. Place the orange halves in the saucepan and add the peppercorns, bay leaves, wine, and salt. Pour enough water over the mixture to cover the orange pieces by ½ inch. Bring to a boil, then reduce the heat to a bare simmer. Cook until the orange peels are tender, about 30 minutes. Drain the oranges, discarding the liquid.

2. SLICE each orange half in half again. Place an orange piece, peel-side down, on a work surface. Scrape or slice off all of the white pith from the peel, discarding the pith. Cut the remaining orange skin into ¼-inch-thick strips. Repeat with the remaining orange pieces. Place the orange peels in a small jar. Pour in enough oil to cover them.

3. SPOON some of the orange confit and oil over the top of grilled or smoked pork slices. The confit will keep in a covered container in the refrigerator for several weeks, but warm it before serving again.

PEANUT COLESLAW

Most pork barbecue sandwiches are simply better with a pile of coleslaw on top of the meat. Some regional slaws are made with a vinegar dressing, some with barbecue sauce mixed in, and some with a basic mayo-based mixture. For something that makes a little statement of its own in the dish, without overwhelming the meat, try this blend. Peanuts have always been considered a fine match for pork. In fact, some Southern hogs used to be grazed on peanuts. MAKES ENOUGH FOR 8 LARGE PORK SANDWICHES

1 cup mayonnaise
1/4 cup plus 2 tablespoons cider vinegar
1/4 cup plus 2 tablespoons granulated sugar
1/2 teaspoon celery salt
1 medium green cabbage head, shredded
2 large carrots, grated
3 tablespoons minced onion
3/4 cup chopped roasted salted peanuts
Kosher salt or coarse salt, optional

1. WHISK together the mayonnaise, vinegar, sugar, and celery salt in a large bowl. Add the cabbage, carrots, and onion and toss together with the dressing. Cover and chill for at least 30 minutes or up to a few hours.

2. JUST BEFORE serving, stir in the salted peanuts. Taste and add salt if needed. Use a slotted spoon to pile the chilled slaw on sandwiches.

BRUSSELS KRAUT

Tangy sweet-sour "kraut" takes on a new guise here but works in many of the same places, since cabbage and Brussels sprouts are cousins in the veggie clan. Pile it atop brats, sausages, or other dogs, or over pulled pork wrapped in a soft flour tortilla. MAKES ABOUT 4 CUPS

> 1 pound Brussels sprouts, shredded
>
> 2 medium carrots, grated
>
> 2 medium celery ribs, finely chopped
>
> 1/2 small red bell pepper, finely chopped
>
> 1/4 cup minced onion
>
> 1 tablespoon kosher salt or coarse sea salt, or more to taste
>
> 2/3 cup granulated sugar
>
> 2/3 cup cider vinegar
>
> 1 tablespoon yellow mustard seeds
>
> 2 tablespoons vegetable oil or sunflower oil

1. PLACE the Brussels sprouts, carrots, celery, bell pepper, and onion in a large heat-proof bowl. Toss with 1 tablespoon salt. Let sit for 30 minutes and then pour off the liquid.

2. COMBINE the sugar, vinegar, and mustard seeds in a saucepan. Warm over medium heat just until the sugar dissolves, stirring a time or two to help it along. Pour the warm sugar-vinegar mixture over the Brussels sprouts mixture. Add the oil and toss together.

3. COOL and then refrigerate in a covered container for at least 1 hour and up to overnight. Taste the mixture to see if it needs more salt, since much of it will have been poured off with the liquid previously. Serve chilled with pork. The mixture will keep in the refrigerator for weeks.

CRANBERRY, FIG, AND PISTACHIO RELISH

FOR GRILLED DISHES

This chilled relish makes quite a festive fall or winter condiment sidled up to a grilled pork loin or tenderloin or with a batch of chops. MAKES ABOUT 3 CUPS

12-ounce package fresh cranberries

1 cup granulated sugar

1 medium orange, peeled and white pith removed, chopped

1/4 cup water

3 tablespoons minced shallots

1 teaspoon ground dried ginger

1 teaspoon yellow mustard seeds

1 teaspoon ground dried mild to medium red chile, such as New Mexican

3/4 teaspoon ground cumin

3/4 teaspoon ground cinnamon

3/4 teaspoon salt

4 ounces dried figs, preferably Mission, chopped

1/3 cup unsalted pistachios, chopped

1. COMBINE the cranberries, sugar, orange and its juice, water, shallots, dried spices, and salt in a saucepan. Cook, uncovered, over medium-high heat, stirring occasionally, until the sugar dissolves and the cranberries pop and thicken, 10 to 15 minutes.

2. STIR in the figs and pistachios and remove from the heat. Cool, then refrigerate in a covered container for at least 1 hour or up to several weeks. Add a little water if it becomes too thick to spoon easily. Serve chilled at the table with pork.

GREEN TOMATO RELISH

In the past most folks thought of green tomatoes as just an end-of-the-season overload. These days, though, they are common at farmers' markets all summer. Of course, any of us who grow our own can always pick a few specimens before they ripen. The tanginess of the tomatoes makes a relish or chowchow a big hit with pork. It's a nice change from coleslaw on a pulled pork sandwich, or serve spoonfuls alongside slices of smoked pork tenderloin. **MAKES ABOUT 4 CUPS**

> 3 pounds green tomatoes, chopped
> 1 medium onion, chopped
> 1 small green bell pepper, seeded and chopped
> 1 tablespoon kosher salt or coarse sea salt
> 3/4 cup packed dark brown sugar
> 3/4 cup cider vinegar
> 1 teaspoon celery seeds
> 1 teaspoon yellow mustard seeds
> 1/2 teaspoon ground dried ginger

1. COMBINE the tomatoes, onion, and bell pepper in a large bowl and toss with the salt. Let sit for 30 minutes, then pour off the liquid. Rinse the vegetables and then drain again.

2. TRANSFER the vegetables to a large saucepan. Add the remaining ingredients and bring the mixture to a boil over medium-high heat. Reduce the heat to a simmer and cook until the mixture has melded together but bits of tomato, onion, and pepper are still distinct, about 15 minutes. Transfer to a bowl or jars, cover, and refrigerate for at least 3 hours or up to 3 weeks before serving.

FRIED SAGE LEAVES

FOR CONTEMPORARY SMOKED FOOD & GRILLED DISHES

Sage, at least the common broadleaf variety, grows especially well in our garden, a big stand of it returning year after year. If we have not managed to kill it, we're sure you can grow it, too. Sage is often paired with chicken or turkey, and it is indeed good there, but we think it has even more to offer with pork. These simply fried leaves turn dark as they fry and look very cool strewn over pork chops or loin or tenderloin slices. **MAKES ENOUGH TO GARNISH 4 TO 6 SERVINGS**

3/4 cup fresh sage leaves
Grapeseed oil or sunflower oil, for frying

1. PLACE a couple of layers of paper towels nearby to drain the sage leaves. Warm ½ inch of oil in a small skillet until it shimmers. Gently place several sage leaves in the oil and fry over medium heat until the leaves stop sizzling and just become crisp, about 20 seconds. Remove the leaves with a slotted spoon and drain on the paper towels.

2. REPEAT until all of the leaves are fried, adjusting the oil temperature downward if the leaves begin to brown before becoming crisp. Serve immediately on pork or hold at room temperature for up to 1 hour.

CHUNKY SALSA VERDE

Here's a quick toss-up to top off pork tacos, sandwiches, or wraps. Other pork will be green with envy. MAKES ABOUT 2 CUPS

> 1 medium cucumber
> 4 ounces tomatillos, chopped
> 1 or 2 fresh jalapeños, seeded and chopped
> Juice of 1/2 lime
> 1 tablespoon vegetable oil or sunflower oil
> 2 to 3 tablespoons minced fresh cilantro
> Kosher salt or coarse sea salt

1. PEEL the cucumber and halve it lengthwise. Scoop out the watery center with a spoon and discard it. Chop the cucumber. Mix the cucumber, tomatillos, jalapeños, lime juice, and vegetable oil in a bowl.

2. STIR in the cilantro and season with salt to taste. Serve at room temperature with smoked or grilled pork.

BEEFING UP
BEEF
AND BISON

DRY RUBS, PASTES, AND MARINADES

SOUTHWESTERN WONDER

FOR TRADITIONAL BARBECUE, CONTEMPORARY SMOKED FOOD, & GRILLED DISHES

Inspired by the flavors of the American Southwest and Mexico, this knockout flavoring mates especially well with steaks that have broad surfaces, such as flank or skirt. MAKES ABOUT 3/4 CUP

1/4 cup cocoa nibs

1/4 cup shelled pumpkin seeds (pepitas), toasted in a dry skillet

1 teaspoon coriander seeds, toasted in a dry skillet

1/4 cup ground dried mild to medium red chile, such as New Mexican

2 teaspoons ground cinnamon

2 teaspoons espresso powder

2 teaspoons kosher salt or coarse sea salt

1 teaspoon ground chipotle chile

1. GRIND together the cocoa nibs, pumpkin seeds, and coriander seeds in a spice grinder or mortar. When finely ground, pour into a small bowl and then mix in the remaining ingredients.

2. SPRINKLE the rub heavily on the beef and then massage it in well. Allow the seasoned meat to sit for at least 45 minutes at room temperature prior to cooking. Store any leftover rub in a covered container in a cool, dark pantry for up to 3 months.

spicing **TIP** Beef and bison don't require strong seasonings to be delicious, but they can handle flavoring blends with chile, chocolate, and coffee, among other hearty tastes.

TOM PERINI'S TEXAS RIBEYE RUB

Tom and his wife, Lisa, run one of the country's best steak joints, the Perini Ranch Steakhouse in Buffalo Gap, a quick boot-scoot from Abilene. You can make up this rub of Tom's by the bucketful if you wish. The cornstarch helps the other seasonings adhere especially well to a steak's surface, contributing to a great grill sear on a ribeye steak, the favorite cut of the Perinis (and the Jamisons). The rub, sprinkled heavily, is a fine choice on any other steak as well. **MAKES ABOUT 2 CUPS**

1 cup coarsely ground black pepper
1/2 cup kosher salt or coarse sea salt
2 tablespoons plus 2 teaspoons cornstarch
2 tablespoons plus 2 teaspoons garlic powder
2 tablespoons plus 2 teaspoons crumbled dried oregano

1. COMBINE all of the ingredients in a small bowl. Press the rub heavily onto the beef. Allow the seasoned meat to sit for at least 45 minutes at room temperature prior to cooking.

2. ANY REMAINING rub can be stored in a covered container in a cool, dark pantry for up to 3 months.

MAGIC MUSHROOM POWDER

Mushrooms offer an elusively wonderful flavor when rubbed onto the surface of a steak or roast. Thyme always goes well with mushrooms, and a little salt helps seal the connection. If you like playing with different salts, this is a good place to try *sel gris*, with its hefty moist crystals and a lingering minerality from gray clay ocean beds. As you might guess from the French name, much of the world's *sel gris* comes from places like Normandy and other coastal areas of France. **MAKES ABOUT 3/4 CUP**

> 2 ounces dried porcini or other dried mushrooms
> 2 teaspoons dried thyme
> 2 tablespoons *sel gris*, kosher salt, or coarse sea salt

1. GRIND together the porcini and thyme in a blender or in batches in a spice grinder. You want a coarse dust. Once they are ground, mix in the *sel gris*. Sprinkle the rub heavily on the beef and then massage it in well. Allow the seasoned meat to sit for at least 45 minutes at room temperature, or up to several hours wrapped or covered in the refrigerator, prior to cooking.

2. STORE any remaining rub in a covered container in a cool, dark pantry for up to 3 months.

spicing **TIP** Mark Bitterman, the sparkplug behind the Meadow, a small collection of delightful salt and flavoring stores in Portland, Oregon, and New York City, says it all started with *sel gris* sprinkled over a steak. Have your own epiphany by checking out atthemeadow.com. The website sells salts and peppers from around the globe, chocolates, other artisanal food products, and the biggest collection of bitters in the world (the guy is named Bitterman, after all). If you invest in *sel gris* from the Meadow or elsewhere, be sure to try a beef or bison steak with nothing more than this salt for flavoring the meat both before and after cooking. The Meadow sells several *sel gris* varieties from France as well as from Vietnam and Slovenia.

CHIMICHURRI DRY RUB

FOR CONTEMPORARY SMOKED FOOD & GRILLED DISHES

Beef's best match at the table just might be chimichurri, the Argentinian slurry of herbs, garlic, and oil. This rub includes the dried versions of chimichurri's key flavors, to flavor the meat before cooking. We like this best on grilled steaks or tender smoked roasts served rare to medium-rare. Make sure the dried herbs are recently purchased, preferably from a spice shop that does a brisk business, so that they have some real character. If you want to double your pleasure, use Black Garlic Chimichurri (page 98) for a table sauce. **MAKES ABOUT 3/4 CUP**

1/4 cup crumbled dried oregano

2 tablespoons dried parsley flakes

2 tablespoons dried summer or winter savory

2 tablespoons crumbled dried thyme

1 tablespoon kosher salt or coarse sea salt

1 tablespoon coarsely ground black pepper

1 tablespoon granulated garlic

1 tablespoon smoked paprika

1. STIR together all of the ingredients in a small bowl. Sprinkle the rub heavily on the beef and then massage it in well.

2. ALLOW the seasoned meat to sit for at least 45 minutes at room temperature, or up to overnight wrapped or covered in the refrigerator, prior to cooking. Store any remaining rub in a covered container in a cool, dark pantry for up to 1 month.

BILL'S BRISKET AND BEEF BLEND

FOR TRADITIONAL BARBECUE & CONTEMPORARY SMOKED FOOD

Bill's roots are as Texan as barbecued brisket itself. After years of experimenting with dry rubs containing chili powder, chiles, cumin, garlic and onion powders, and more, he's gone back pretty much to the basics. A little garlic salt ups the complexity of elemental salt and pepper just a touch, adding a rounder note to the blend than garlic powder. This batch makes enough to smear a good-size packer-trim brisket and alchemize it into the food of the gods. It's excellent on a smoked beef tenderloin, too. If a sauce is desired for either, try Texas Black Gold (page 94). **MAKES ABOUT 1 CUP**

> 1/2 cup freshly ground black pepper, preferably Tellicherry
> 1/2 cup kosher salt or coarse sea salt
> 1/4 cup garlic salt

1. COMBINE all of the ingredients in a small bowl. Sprinkle the rub heavily on the beef and then massage it in well.

2. ALLOW the seasoned meat to sit for at least 45 minutes at room temperature, or up to overnight wrapped or covered in the refrigerator, prior to cooking. Any remaining rub can be stored in a covered container in a cool, dark pantry for up to 3 months.

spicing **TIP** With notable exceptions like teriyaki marinades and ketchup used as a finishing sauce, beef and bison shine most smartly without sugar in flavoring blends. Sometimes a small amount might be helpful for caramelizing the surface of meat but, generally, forget sugar, honey, molasses, corn syrup, and such when flavoring these meats.

WORCESTERSHIRE DUST

FOR GRILLED DISHES

Dehydrated Worcestershire sauce concentrates the savory complexity of this classic sauce. It's potent stuff on its own, so we don't gussy it up too much in this dry rub, which is great on a burger, kebab, or steak. MAKES ABOUT ½ CUP

> ¼ cup Worcestershire powder
> 2 tablespoons garlic salt
> 2 tablespoons kosher salt or coarse sea salt
> 2 tablespoons sweet paprika
> 2 tablespoons dried mustard powder

1. STIR together all of the ingredients in a small bowl. Sprinkle the rub heavily on the beef and then massage it in well.

2. ALLOW the seasoned meat to sit for at least 45 minutes at room temperature prior to cooking. Store any leftover rub in a covered container in a cool, dark pantry for up to 3 months.

spicing **TIP** **If you can't find Worcestershire powder locally, look for it online from Pendery's World of Chiles & Spices in Fort Worth (penderys. com). The company's been in business since the 1800s.**

LEMON-SHALLOT SALT

If you own a dehydrator, you probably use it to make condiments like this regularly. However, you don't really need special equipment to put together this rub—just a little help from the sun, oven, or grill. This rub brightens any steak, but we particularly like it sprinkled on the Tuscan T-bone or porterhouse steak called *bistecca alla fiorentina*, a hearty charred steak topped with olive oil, lemon juice, and arugula. MAKES ABOUT 1/2 CUP

> 1 large shallot, minced
> 2 tablespoons fresh lemon zest (from 2 large lemons)
> 1/3 cup kosher salt or coarse sea salt

1. **DRY** the shallot and lemon zest. On a hot summer day with low humidity, this can be accomplished by setting the shallot and lemon zest on a plate and leaving it in the sun for an hour. Cover it lightly with cheesecloth if insects are an issue. Otherwise, sprinkle the shallot and lemon zest on a small piece of heavy-duty foil and place in a 200°F oven or on a low grill until dry, about 30 minutes.

2. **COMBINE** the dried shallot and lemon zest with the salt in a small jar or other covered container. Let it sit for at least a day for the flavors to meld and use within a few weeks for the most intense taste. Sprinkle the rub heavily on the beef and then massage it in well. Allow the seasoned meat to sit for at least 45 minutes at room temperature prior to cooking.

GREEN AND BLACK PEPPERCORN SLATHER

FOR TRADITIONAL BARBECUE & CONTEMPORARY SMOKED FOOD

According to a recent survey, many people have the mistaken impression that a green peppercorn and a caper are the same thing. Not even close, though both are often sold in jars in brine, and they may be found near each other in the supermarket. Make sure to get pungent young peppercorns for this paste. It's a little too heady to massage fully onto a grilled steak or other small piece of beef, but it balances well with the heavier flavor of smoke.

MAKES ABOUT 2/3 CUP

1/4 cup drained green peppercorns

1/4 cup cracked black peppercorns

2 tablespoons kosher salt or coarse sea salt

1. PLACE all of the ingredients in a spice grinder and pulse a few times, just enough to break down the peppercorns a bit. You want a coarse, moist mixture. Cover and store in the refrigerator if you're not using it the same day it's made.

2. MASSAGE the paste heavily on the beef. Allow the seasoned meat to sit for at least 45 minutes at room temperature, or up to overnight wrapped or covered in the refrigerator, prior to cooking.

spicing TIP Keep in mind that the wood you cook over is, in essence, a seasoning, too. If you cook with logs, you may be limited by expense to what hardwood grows in your area. But you can still get some finishing woods, smaller pieces or even pellets that you can throw into the fire to amp up certain qualities. We use cherry trimmings ourselves, since we have cherry trees in our yard that are not sprayed with anything toxic. Other fruit woods, like apple, peach, and fig, are good prospects for their sweet smoke, as are grapevines if you happen to have them in abundance. Nut woods like pecan can be softer and smoother than assertive hickory and black walnut. Mesquite's a hot wood in all respects, but much better for quick high-heat grilling than for slow barbecuing because the smoke tends to turn bitter over long periods.

ITALIAN STEAK PASTE

FOR CONTEMPORARY SMOKED FOOD & GRILLED DISHES

A South Omaha tradition since 1934, Piccolo Pete's Italian steakhouse provides the inspiration for this flavorful crust. Our version of the recipe makes enough to smear over a 5-pound prime rib, a couple of porterhouses, or a quartet of ribeyes. If you want a sterling final flourish at the table, consider Charred Scallion and Pink Peppercorn Vinaigrette (page 104). MAKES ABOUT 1 CUP

> 1 large garlic head (about 15 cloves), peeled
> 1/4 cup coarsely ground black pepper
> 3 tablespoons dried basil
> 2 tablespoons dried oregano
> 1 tablespoon dried mustard powder
> 1 tablespoon kosher salt or coarse sea salt
> 1 1/2 teaspoons celery salt

1. **PLACE** all of the ingredients in a food processor and puree. Use right away or cover and refrigerate for up to several days. Massage the paste heavily onto the beef.

2. **ALLOW** the seasoned meat to sit for at least 45 minutes at room temperature, or up to overnight wrapped or covered in the refrigerator, prior to cooking.

UMAMI BOMB

FOR GRILLED DISHES

The Bomb is full of earthy soy sauce and miso, marinade ingredients recognized for their super-savoriness, or umami, sometimes described as the fifth taste. Try this on flat-iron, flank, or hanger steak, and bite-size beef skewers. We mention a couple of optional piquant Japanese spice blends you can add, too, if you wish. If you decide to use *shichimi togarashi*, sprinkle a little over the finished dish as well. **MAKES ABOUT 1³/₄ CUPS**

1/4 cup plus 2 tablespoons red miso
1/4 cup soy sauce
1/4 cup water
2 tablespoons mirin
2 tablespoons packed brown sugar
1 teaspoon *shichimi togarashi* or *yuzu kosho* (see Spicing Tip), optional

1. COMBINE the miso, soy, water, mirin, and brown sugar in a blender and puree. If you are using the *shichimi togarashi*, stir it in now. The marinade can sit at room temperature for a few hours, but refrigerate it in a covered container if you are not planning to use it within that amount of time.

2. POUR the marinade over the meat and refrigerate wrapped or covered for at least 2 hours and up to 8 hours prior to cooking.

spicing **TIP** *Shichimi togarashi* mixes sesame with chile, seaweed, dried ginger, and other flavorings and is sometimes referred to as a Japanese seven-spice powder. *Yuzu kosho* combines chile and the minced peel from yuzu, an orange-like citrus fruit, and ferments the mixture. Look for them in a well-stocked spice section, spice shop, Asian grocery, or online source.

HEARTY HERB MARINADE

FOR TRADITIONAL BARBECUE, CONTEMPORARY SMOKED FOOD, & GRILLED DISHES

This is about as close as we get to the idea of bottled Italian salad dressing, the well-known secret behind a lot of prize-winning barbecue. This marinade is seasoned with red meat in mind, and is enough to soak a tenderloin for four diners, or perhaps a pair of flat-iron steaks. Roasting the garlic mellows the flavor, making it the perfect natural thickener to ensure the marinade will cling to the meat. MAKES ABOUT 1½ CUPS

1 large garlic head
1/2 cup extra-virgin olive oil
1/4 cup red wine vinegar
2 tablespoons water
2 teaspoons dried rosemary
2 teaspoons dried oregano
1 teaspoon kosher salt or coarse sea salt
1/4 teaspoon granulated sugar

1. PREHEAT the oven to 350°F. Wrap the garlic head in foil and bake it until the individual garlic cloves are soft, 50 to 60 minutes. Unwrap and, when cool enough to handle, pop each garlic clove out of its skin.

2. PLACE the garlic and all remaining ingredients in a blender and puree. Use the marinade right away or store in a covered container in the refrigerator for up to a week.

3. POUR the marinade over the beef and marinate for as little as 30 minutes at room temperature or up to overnight, wrapped or covered in the refrigerator, with the lesser time adequate for grilling and the longer time helpful for barbecuing.

BEER AND CITRUS MARINADE

Steaks with broad surfaces relative to thickness take to marinades like ducks to a pond. Use this on skirt steaks, flank, or other "lesser" cuts of beef. Whip it up just before you plan to marinate your beef. We often turn grilled skirt or flank steak into fajitas, then serve the meat with Serrano Pico de Gallo (page 107). MAKES ABOUT 2 CUPS

> 12-ounce bottle or can beer, perhaps hearty Mexican beer
> 3-ounce can frozen orange juice concentrate, thawed
> Juice of 2 large limes
> 1 tablespoon Worcestershire sauce
> 1 teaspoon kosher salt or coarse sea salt

1. COMBINE all of the ingredients in a medium-size bowl and stir well.

2. POUR the marinade over the meat and refrigerate wrapped or covered for at least 2 hours and up to 8 hours prior to cooking.

KOREAN MARINADE

A flanken rib, an amazing little feat of butchery, is created by a crosscut from the chuck end of the short ribs. The knife work results in long strips of meat with just a small section of bone atop each. It's a common cut in Asian markets, and any other meat market worthy of its name can prepare it for you, too. We mention flanken here because it's the perfect cut to immerse in this explosive flavoring. Sirloin also laps it up fabulously. If you plan to barbecue the meat, make the marinade a day ahead so that your beef can have an overnight soak for the fullest taste. This batch makes enough for 4 to 5 pounds of meat. MAKES ABOUT 2¼ CUPS

> 1½ cups *ganjang* (Korean soy sauce) or Japanese soy sauce, such as Kikkoman
> ¼ cup plus 2 tablespoons packed light brown sugar
> ¼ cup Asian sesame oil
> 2 tablespoons *gochujang* (Korean red pepper paste or sauce) or sriracha, optional
> 6 to 8 garlic cloves

1. COMBINE the marinade ingredients in a blender or food processor and blitz until a smooth, thick puree forms.

2. POUR the marinade over the meat and refrigerate, wrapped or covered, from 2 hours to overnight, with the lesser time adequate for grilling and the longer time helpful for barbecuing. If possible, turn the meat in the marinade a time or two.

spicing **TIP** Do you want to be prepared to spice most anything, most any time? Your pantry should include specialty items for cuisine styles you like, such as these Korean condiments if you're a fan of the flavors. Other core ingredients you need include olive oil, at least one type of Tabasco sauce, Worcestershire sauce, red wine vinegar, white or cider vinegar, Dijon mustard, yellow mustard, dried mild red chiles, and dried hot red chiles.

WASABI-YAKI MARINADE

FOR GRILLED DISHES

Teriyaki is a superb seasoning with its sweet and tangy tones. Adding wasabi to the mix makes it vibrate with flavor. If you have a favorite commercial teriyaki sauce, you can use it, but cut it with some vinegar, too, so that it doesn't burn as a marinade. Use this on teriyaki-type skewers of top sirloin or tenderloin, or even on a New York strip steak. MAKES ABOUT 1½ CUPS

1/2 cup Japanese soy sauce, such as Kikkoman

1/2 cup mirin

1/4 cup sake or dry sherry

2 tablespoons minced fresh ginger

1 tablespoon granulated sugar

2 garlic cloves, minced

1/2 teaspoon wasabi (Japanese horseradish) paste, or more to taste

1. STIR together the soy sauce, mirin, sake, ginger, sugar, and garlic in a medium-size bowl until the sugar has dissolved. Add wasabi paste to taste—make it quite bold in flavor at this point because the impact will mellow on the meat.

2. POUR the marinade over the beef. Meat for skewers can soak for as little as 30 minutes at room temperature prior to cooking. A bigger steak can bathe in the marinade wrapped or covered in the refrigerator for up to 8 hours.

THE EYE-OPENER

Like most marinades, this one is especially good on the broad surfaces of flank, skirt, or sirloin steak. The quantity of Tabasco leaves behind a strong hit of flavor, but not a scorching amount of heat. MAKES ABOUT 1¾ CUPS

1½ cups strong brewed coffee

2 tablespoons Tabasco sauce, preferably Original Red or Chipotle, or other hot pepper sauce

1 tablespoon packed brown sugar

1 teaspoon kosher salt or coarse sea salt

1 teaspoon freshly ground black pepper

1. COMBINE all of the ingredients in a small bowl. Use the marinade right away or store in a covered container in the refrigerator for up to a week.

2. POUR the marinade over the beef and marinate for as little as 30 minutes at room temperature or up to overnight, wrapped or covered in the refrigerator, with the lesser time adequate for grilling and the longer time helpful for smoking.

spicing **TIP** Bourbon. It's a one-ingredient wonder. Simply soak a strip or T-bone steak in a bourbon bath. Dry off the surface (to avoid creating an alcohol-stoked bonfire) and pat the meat down with coarse salt and pepper before cooking.

TIPSY TENDERLOIN MARINADE

Strong flavors help amp up mildly meaty beef tenderloin, and a touch of oil helps keep the lean meat from drying out. MAKES ABOUT 1¹/₂ CUPS

> 1 cup brandy
> ¹/₄ cup brown mustard
> 2 tablespoons Worcestershire sauce
> 1 tablespoon vegetable oil or sunflower oil
> 1 tablespoon cracked black peppercorns
> 1 teaspoon kosher salt or coarse sea salt

1. WHISK together all of the ingredients in a medium-size bowl. Use the marinade right away or store in a covered container in the refrigerator for up to a week.

2. POUR the marinade over the beef and marinate for as little as 30 minutes at room temperature or up to overnight, wrapped or covered in the refrigerator, with the lesser time adequate for grilling and the longer time helpful for smoking.

RED WINE AND SOY SOAK

The initial recommendation for this combo came from the folks at the Edna Valley Vineyard, a favorite winery of ours on the California central coast. Their wine of choice in the marinade is their own Meritage, a tasty blend of Merlot, Cabernet, and Petit Verdot. MAKES ABOUT 1³/₄ CUPS

3/4 cup dry red wine

3/4 cup soy sauce

2 tablespoons Dijon mustard

2 tablespoons cracked black pepper

2 garlic cloves, minced

1. WHISK together all of the ingredients in a small bowl. Use right away or refrigerate in a covered container for a day or two.

2. POUR the marinade over the beef and marinate for as little as 30 minutes at room temperature or up to overnight, wrapped or covered in the refrigerator, with the lesser time adequate for grilling and the longer time helpful for smoking.

MOPS AND BASTES

JALAPEÑO-BEER MOP

FOR TRADITIONAL BARBECUE

This is our go-to Texas brisket mop, which continues the flavoring work after an initial rub with Bill's Brisket and Beef Blend (page 75). Try it on barbecued burgers or beef short ribs, too. MAKES ABOUT 4 CUPS

12-ounce bottle or can medium-bodied beer

1 cup cider vinegar or liquid from a jar of pickled jalapeños or pickled peppers

1/2 cup sliced pickled or fresh jalapeños

1/2 cup water

1/4 cup vegetable oil

1/2 medium onion, chopped or sliced in thin rings

2 tablespoons Worcestershire sauce

1 to 2 tablespoons Bill's Brisket and Beef Blend (page 75) *or* 2 teaspoons kosher salt or coarse sea salt plus 2 teaspoons coarse-ground black pepper

1. **COMBINE** all of the ingredients in a medium-size saucepan.

2. **HEAT** the mop before you plan to use it initially and keep it warm over low heat between bastes. Apply to the meat about once an hour.

WALTER JETTON'S BARBECUE MOP

FOR TRADITIONAL BARBECUE

Walter Jetton catered Lyndon B. Johnson's legendary barbecues at his Texas ranch and in Washington. Mr. Jetton, an old-school master of the craft, published a book in 1965 called, appropriately enough, *Walter Jetton's LBJ Barbecue Cookbook*. The inspiration for this mop was his sole one in the small book and may have been the first time that any barbecue cook actually put a mop recipe into print. The original recipe made enough mop to swab down a whole cow. The quantity here is still big enough for a sizeable event, but you can cut the recipe in half if you are cooking a single beef brisket or shoulder, or a batch of short ribs. **MAKES ABOUT 3 QUARTS**

2 quarts beef stock

2 cups Worcestershire sauce

1 cup vinegar

1 cup vegetable oil

1¹/₂ tablespoons kosher salt or coarse sea salt

1¹/₂ tablespoons dried mustard powder

1¹/₂ tablespoons sweet paprika

1 tablespoon garlic powder

1 tablespoon chili powder

1 tablespoon Tabasco sauce or other Louisiana hot sauce

1 bay leaf

1. COMBINE all of the ingredients in a stockpot. Mr. Jetton recommended letting the mop sit overnight. If your refrigerator lacks room for that, just make it up right before you begin to cook.

2. HEAT the mop before you plan to use it initially and keep it warm over low heat between bastes. Apply to the meat about once an hour.

BOURBON SOP

As we mentioned previously, we use bourbon alone as a quick and easy marinade for beef. This mop for barbecue and other smoke-cooking benefits from some of the same spirit and a little added complexity. **MAKES ABOUT 3 CUPS**

> $1^1/2$ cups inexpensive bourbon or other whiskey
> $1/2$ cup white vinegar
> $1/2$ cup water
> $1/4$ cup vegetable oil
> $1/2$ medium onion, chopped
> 1 tablespoon steak sauce, such as A.1. Original
> 1 teaspoon kosher salt or coarse sea salt
> 1 teaspoon ground black pepper

1. COMBINE all of the ingredients in a saucepan.

2. HEAT the mop before you plan to use it initially and keep it warm over low heat between bastes. Apply to the meat about once an hour.

> VARIATION: Turn this mop into a red wine and butter splash by switching out the bourbon for dry red wine and the oil for unsalted butter.

spicing TIP   Unlike smoke-cooked beef, grilled beef benefits little from basting. The most you might want to do is brush melted butter on a steak near the end of the cooking time.

SAUCES

KOREAN BARBECUE SAUCE

FOR TRADITIONAL BARBECUE, CONTEMPORARY SMOKED FOOD, & GRILLED DISHES

You can slather this on in the last stages of cooking smoked or grilled beef ribs, especially flanken ribs, but we use it mainly as a table sauce for ribs or lettuce wraps. It's made to go with our Korean Marinade (page 84).

MAKES ABOUT 2 CUPS

1 1/2 cups *ganjang* (Korean soy sauce) or Japanese soy sauce, such as Kikkoman

1/2 cup ketchup

1/2 cup rice vinegar

1/4 cup packed light brown sugar

1/4 cup sliced scallions

2 tablespoons Asian sesame oil

2 tablespoons *gochujang* (Korean red pepper paste or sauce) or sriracha, optional

1 tablespoon minced fresh ginger

3 garlic cloves, minced

1. COMBINE all of the ingredients in a saucepan over medium heat. When the mixture reaches a simmer, reduce the heat to medium-low and cook until reduced by about one-third, 15 to 20 minutes.

2. USE SOME of the sauce warm as a baste in the last few minutes of cooking, if you wish, and serve more at the table with the food. The sauce will keep in a covered container in the refrigerator for at least 2 weeks, but reheat it before serving.

TEXAS BLACK GOLD

FOR TRADITIONAL BARBECUE, CONTEMPORARY SMOKED FOOD, & GRILLED DISHES

Dark and lustrous, and piquant from black pepper, this sauce has a mellow background of tomato without too much sweetness. Well-smoked brisket, short ribs, and other Texas barbecue never really require sauce, but this one is always welcome on our table. If you have any meat drippings from whatever you are cooking, mix them into the sauce before serving. MAKES ABOUT 3 CUPS

> 4 tablespoons (1/2 stick) unsalted butter
> 2 cups minced sweet onion
> 1/4 cup packed dark brown sugar
> 1 cup water
> 1 cup ketchup
> 1/4 cup cider vinegar
> 3 tablespoons Worcestershire sauce
> 2 tablespoons cracked black peppercorns
> 1 teaspoon freshly ground black pepper
> 1 teaspoon kosher salt or coarse sea salt, or more to taste
> 1 teaspoon liquid smoke (see Spicing Tip), optional

1. WARM the butter in a saucepan over medium-low heat. Stir in the onion bits and sauté slowly until they are quite soft and beginning to turn golden, 12 to 15 minutes. Stir the onions frequently after they begin to soften. Mix in the brown sugar and cook for several minutes more to caramelize some of the onion bits.

2. STIR in the remaining ingredients and bring the sauce to a simmer. Cover and cook for 30 minutes, then allow the sauce to cool briefly. We like this sauce on the thin side, so it can easily dribble off the spoon. If it's too thick, stir in a tablespoon or two of water.

3. SERVE the sauce at the table warm or chilled with any cut of beef. Stored in a covered container, it will keep refrigerated for at least a week.

spicing **TIP** **Liquid smoke contributes a certain basic distilled smoke taste to anything it's stirred into. However, our preferred method for adding**

smoke flavor is to stick a pot of sauce or another dish right into the smoker when it's already fired up. It's one of those little touches of showmanship that impress the heck out of guests.

NORTEÑO SALSA DE ARBOL Y TOMATILLOS

FOR GRILLED DISHES

This classic table sauce features the roasty, toasty notes of both dried red chiles and tomatillos. It's perfect for beef tacos and burritos or a grilled Mexican-style steak. MAKES ABOUT 2 CUPS

> 10 to 12 whole chiles de árbol, stems broken off and loose seeds discarded
>
> 1 pound whole tomatillos
>
> 1/2 cup water
>
> 2 tablespoons chopped fresh cilantro, optional
>
> 2 or 3 garlic cloves
>
> 1 teaspoon freshly squeezed lime juice
>
> 1/2 teaspoon kosher salt or coarse sea salt

1. WARM a griddle or cast-iron skillet over medium heat. Place the chiles on the griddle, in batches if necessary. As soon as they begin to get fragrant—a matter of seconds— turn them over and toast them briefly on the second side. Remove them quickly from the griddle so they don't burn. Place the whole tomatillos on the griddle and roast them, turning them so that they color somewhat evenly, 6 to 8 minutes.

2. PLOP the chiles and tomatillos into a blender with the remaining ingredients. Puree, adding a bit more water if the mixture is too thick to spoon easily. Use the salsa right away or refrigerate in a covered container for 1 hour to allow the flavors to mingle more. Serve the salsa at room temperature or chilled at the table alongside the food. Leftover salsa will keep in the refrigerator for a few days, but its zip begins to fade.

BROWN SUGAR–ANISE BARBECUE SAUCE

Mildly sweet and redolent of licorice-like ground anise, this sauce seems both familiar and mysterious at the same time. It's terrific on barbecued beef short ribs or even a grilled burger—beef or bison. MAKES ABOUT 2 CUPS

1¹/2 cups ketchup

1 cup water

³/4 cup cider vinegar

¹/4 cup minced fresh cilantro

¹/4 cup packed brown sugar

2 tablespoons Worcestershire sauce

2 garlic cloves, minced

2 teaspoons ground anise

1¹/2 teaspoons kosher salt or coarse sea salt

1 teaspoon Tabasco sauce or other hot pepper sauce

¹/2 teaspoon ground cumin

1. MIX all of the ingredients in a medium-size saucepan and bring to a simmer over medium-high heat. Reduce the heat to low and cook the mixture, stirring frequently, until it thickens and reduces by about one-third, 35 to 40 minutes.

2. SERVE the sauce warm on or alongside the meat. It will keep in a covered container in the refrigerator for at least 2 weeks, but reheat it before serving.

BLACK GARLIC CHIMICHURRI

FOR GRILLED DISHES

Juan Bochenski, executive chef of Santa Fe's Rosewood Inn of the Anasazi, is a native of Buenos Aires. He whips up all kinds of tangy chimichurri herb sauces, Argentina's favorite accompaniment to steak. We always can count on them being delicious, but beyond parsley you never know what might show up in the oil-and-vinegar-based condiment. He inspired our take on chimichurri here, where fermented black garlic, traditionally an Asian ingredient, is used to flavor the sauce. You might guess that a fresh herb sauce would be best right after it's made, but chimichurri should actually be allowed to sit in the refrigerator for at least a few hours, and preferably a day, for the flavors to blend. Lavish the sauce over any grilled cuts of beef or bison.

MAKES ABOUT 2 CUPS

1/4 cup red wine vinegar

1/4 cup water

2 teaspoons kosher salt or coarse sea salt

1 black garlic head, cloves peeled and mashed (see Spicing Tip)

1 cup fresh flat-leaf parsley leaves, finely minced

1/2 cup fresh oregano leaves, finely minced

1/4 cup fresh mint leaves, finely minced

1 teaspoon crushed hot red chile flakes

1/2 cup extra-virgin olive oil

1. WHISK together the vinegar, water, and salt in a bowl. When the salt has dissolved, whisk in the garlic, parsley, oregano, mint, and chile. Then whisk in the oil.

2. POUR the sauce into a covered container and refrigerate for at least 3 hours or up to 2 weeks. Serve chilled alongside meat for diners to enjoy to their taste.

spicing **TIP** During black garlic's fermenting process, it darkens and becomes sweeter and mellower. Look for black garlic these days at Trader Joe's, many other supermarkets, and online. It keeps for weeks in a cool, dark pantry. You can use a regular head of garlic, very finely minced, for this sauce, but the sauce will have a slightly sharper taste.

ARGENTINE SALSA CRIOLLA

FOR TRADITIONAL BARBECUE, CONTEMPORARY SMOKED FOOD, & GRILLED DISHES

Since Argentinians eat more beef even than Americans, it makes sense to offer a second sauce familiar on tables there. Some versions emphasize tomatoes more than bell peppers, others the opposite. We like something of a balance. *Salsa criolla* is delightful spooned on everything from brisket to a New York strip steak or even a burger. **MAKES ABOUT 2 CUPS**

> 8 ounces ripe red tomatoes, seeded, squeezed of watery liquid, and very finely diced
> 1 small red bell pepper, seeded and very finely diced
> 1 small yellow bell pepper, seeded and very finely diced
> 1/2 medium red or white onion, minced
> 1/4 cup red wine vinegar
> 1 teaspoon kosher salt or coarse sea salt
> 1/2 cup extra-virgin olive oil
> 1/2 teaspoon crushed hot red chile flakes, optional

1. MIX all of the ingredients in a bowl. Refrigerate the salsa in a covered container for a minimum of 1 hour and preferably several hours, or up to a week.

2. LET THE salsa sit at room temperature for about 30 minutes before using, spooned over beef or bison.

SALSA GOLF

A simply stirred-together mixture of mayonnaise and ketchup serves as the basis for all kinds of "secret" sauces. With names like fry sauce, especially big in Utah, and the come-back or cumback sauce of the South, the blends boost burgers, dogs, and sometimes even iceberg salads. Here's the version that reigns throughout many areas of Latin America. The name reputedly comes from its genesis in an upscale golf club. **MAKES ABOUT 1 1/2 CUPS**

> 1 cup mayonnaise
> 3 tablespoons ketchup
> 1 1/2 teaspoons Worcestershire sauce
> Squeeze of lemon juice

1. STIR together all of the ingredients in a small bowl. Use immediately or refrigerate the salsa in a covered container for up to 3 weeks.

2. SPOON the salsa, at room temperature or chilled, over burgers or other beef.

VARIATION: Stir up to 1/3 cup sweet pickle relish into the sauce.

CINNAMON RED HOT KETCHUP

If you're a ketchup fan, this could become your burger's best friend. We keep the sugar at a moderate level so that the cinnamon and chile flavors come through. **MAKES ABOUT 2 CUPS**

1 tablespoon vegetable oil or sunflower oil

1/2 cup minced onion

14- to 15-ounce can diced tomatoes with juice

1 cup rice vinegar

3/4 cup apple cider or juice

2 tablespoons packed brown sugar

2 tablespoons light corn syrup

1 tablespoon ground cinnamon

1 tablespoon ground dried hot red chile, such as New Mexican

1 teaspoon Tabasco sauce

1 teaspoon kosher salt or coarse sea salt, or more to taste

1. WARM the oil in a large saucepan over medium heat. Stir in the onion and sauté until translucent and beginning to soften, about 5 minutes. Add the remaining ingredients and bring to a boil. Reduce the heat to low and cook for about 45 minutes to blend the flavors and thicken the liquid. Let the mixture cool briefly.

2. SCRAPE the mixture into a blender or food processor and puree it. Pour the ketchup into a jar, bottle, or other covered container. The ketchup keeps refrigerated for several weeks. Serve chilled along with any food that ketchup can bless.

GREEN CHILE–TEQUILA SAUCE

The idea here is based on New Mexico's beloved green chile sauce, but we kick it up an extra notch with tequila. The sauce is meant to accompany grilled steaks, barbecued brisket, or most any other cut of beef or bison.

MAKES ABOUT 2^1/$_2$ CUPS

2 tablespoons vegetable oil

^{1}/$_2$ medium onion, finely chopped

2 garlic cloves, minced

1 tablespoon all-purpose flour

^{1}/$_3$ cup tequila

1 cup chicken or beef stock

2 cups chopped roasted mild to medium-hot New Mexican green chiles, fresh or thawed frozen

^{1}/$_2$ teaspoon kosher salt or coarse sea salt, or more to taste

1. WARM the oil in a heavy saucepan over medium heat. Add the onion and garlic and sauté until the onion is soft and translucent, about 7 minutes. Stir in the flour and continue cooking for another 1 or 2 minutes.

2. POUR in the tequila, scraping up from the bottom. Immediately begin pouring in the stock, stirring as you go. Mix in the chiles and then the salt. Bring the mixture to a boil. Reduce the heat to a low simmer and cook until the sauce is thickened but still very pourable, about 15 minutes.

3. SERVE warm at the table or refrigerate in a covered container for later use. The sauce keeps for up to 1 week, but reheat it before serving.

CHARRED SCALLION AND PINK PEPPERCORN VINAIGRETTE

FOR GRILLED DISHES

Charring vegetables and turning them into an ingredient isn't a new idea, despite recently revived enthusiasm for the technique among chefs. If you're firing up your grill anyway, just char the scallions over the fire. Otherwise, you can do the charring in a heavy skillet, or on a griddle or plancha. Spoon this vinaigrette over everything from a sizzling prime porterhouse to a humbler but also scrumptious flank steak. It also enhances grilled eggplant slices and other vegetables. The vinaigrette is best made shortly before serving.

MAKES ABOUT 1 CUP

1/2 cup extra-virgin olive oil

8 to 10 scallions, roots and any limp green portions trimmed

2 tablespoons fresh lemon juice

1 tablespoon rice vinegar

1 teaspoon Dijon mustard

2 teaspoons pink peppercorns, roughly cracked

1/2 teaspoon kosher salt or coarse sea salt, or more to taste

1. **USE** about 1 teaspoon of the oil to rub the scallions. Char the scallions by your preferred method (see above) until they are somewhat blackened and partially soft. Place the warm scallions on a piece of plastic wrap, cover them, and let them steam to soften further. When they are cool, cut the scallions on the bias as neatly as possible into ½-inch pieces.

2. **WHISK** the remaining oil with the lemon juice, vinegar, and mustard in a bowl. When combined, whisk in the scallion pieces, peppercorns, and salt. Serve warm, spooned over beef, or let cool to room temperature before using.

spicing **TIP** A few pink peppercorns can be rubbed between your fingers and crumbled. When you want more than a teaspoon, place the peppercorns in a plastic bag and crush with a spoon.

OTHER CONDIMENTS FOR FLAVORING

FRESH HORSERADISH AIOLI

FOR GRILLED DISHES

A decent horseradish sauce for beef is as simple as stirring together prepared horseradish with sour cream. When you want to impress your guests a bit more, whip together this garlicky mayo with the fresh-grated root. Serve it alongside a ribeye that has been flavored with Tom Perini's Texas Ribeye Rub (page 71). MAKES ABOUT 1½ CUPS

6 to 8 garlic cloves

3/4 teaspoon kosher salt or coarse sea salt, or more to taste

1 large egg and 2 large egg yolks, at room temperature

1/2 teaspoon fresh lemon juice

1/2 cup vegetable oil or sunflower oil

1/2 cup extra-virgin olive oil

2 tablespoons freshly grated horseradish, or more to taste

1. CRUSH together the garlic and salt in a small mortar. Scrape up the mixture and transfer to a food processor.

2. ADD to the processor the egg, egg yolks, and lemon juice. With the processor running, drizzle in the vegetable oil, followed by the olive oil. When a fluffy mayonnaise-like emulsion forms, stop and stir in the horseradish. Taste and see if more salt is needed. Serve a spoonful on top of, or beside, a steak.

SYRAH FINISHING SALT

This gorgeous, nearly purple salt is meant to scatter over meat on the plate, a final flourish to show your guests your taste is as good as your cooking cred. The infused salt, inspired by others on the market today, is just one of many you can make with the same technique explained here. We have selected the wine—Syrah—that we most enjoy with red meat. However, you could switch it out for a Cabernet, a Malbec, or a dry red blend. It's easy to double or otherwise increase the size of the batch. A jar of this makes a nice gift to other cooks. Because the cooking time is a number of hours, you might want to make this overnight in the oven, or plan to do it some other time that the oven doesn't need to be in use. And if you have a convection oven, use it for this. Of course, if you live somewhere as dry as we do, you can set this out in the summer for a full day and let solar heat do the work of the oven. Save it for a grilled beef dish or one that is quickly smoke-cooked rather than serious barbecue, where it would be a little lost. **MAKES ABOUT 1 CUP**

> 1 cup kosher salt or coarse sea salt
>
> 1/4 cup plus 2 tablespoons Syrah or a red blend containing Syrah, such as a Côtes du Rhône

1. PREHEAT the oven to 200°F. Cut a piece of parchment paper to fit a baking sheet.

2. STIR the salt and wine together in a small bowl. You'll have a slurry almost immediately. Spread the mixture in a thin layer on the baking sheet. Bake the salt in the oven until dry, about 8 hours in a convection oven and maybe up to 12 hours in a conventional oven. The salt will recrystallize. If you wish to have a finer salt, grind it in a spice grinder, in batches if necessary.

3. STORE the salt in a covered container at room temperature for up to 2 months. The flavor and color will gradually fade. Sprinkle over dinner in the same way you would with any other salt.

We think a lot of simple finishing fillips can rev up a quality dish to a stellar level in presentation and taste. The wine salt is a fine example, but so are the array of finishing salts available in spice stores and other retail outlets today. If you want to experiment with flavored salts without taking the time to mix and evaporate your own, check out the Meadow (see the Spicing Tip on page 72). Of course, you can also opt for an extra-flaky salt like Maldon, the fabulous British sea salt sold today in most well-stocked supermarkets, or French *fleur de sel*, found in most specialty spice stores. Other easy flourishes include grilled lemon or lime wedges, a few drops of aged balsamic, high-quality extra-virgin olive oil or pumpkin seed oil, cracked peppercorns of varied colors, sunflower kernels, pepitas (hulled pumpkin seeds), bread crumbs, and even gingerbread crumbs.

SERRANO PICO DE GALLO

FOR TRADITIONAL BARBECUE, CONTEMPORARY SMOKED FOOD, & GRILLED DISHES

A zippy, fresh salsa to enliven any beef bash. MAKES ABOUT 2 CUPS

1 pound plum tomatoes
3 or 4 fresh serrano chiles, seeded and minced
1/4 cup minced white onion
1/4 cup chopped fresh cilantro
Juice of 1/2 lime
1/2 teaspoon kosher salt or coarse sea salt, or more to taste

1. MIX all of the ingredients in a medium-size bowl. Let sit at room temperature for about 30 minutes.

2. SERVE at room temperature or chilled, preferably the same day, spooned over nearly any cut of beef.

VIETNAMESE-STYLE CARROT-DAIKON RELISH

FOR TRADITIONAL BARBECUE, CONTEMPORARY SMOKED FOOD, & GRILLED DISHES

Essentially a quick pickle, matchsticks of carrots and daikon add sweetness and crunch to grilled beef skewers or grilled beef in a Vietnamese-style *bánh mì* sandwich. Try the relish on a barbecued brisket sandwich instead of dill pickles, or toss it together with steak slices and a few torn greens for a great lunch salad. Adjust the quantities of carrots and mild Asian daikon radish up or down as you wish. Julienne the vegetables in a food processor to speed up the prep. **MAKES ABOUT 3 CUPS**

> 8 ounces carrots, cut into matchsticks
> 8 ounces daikon radish, cut into matchsticks
> 3/4 cup rice vinegar
> 1/4 cup plus 2 tablespoons granulated sugar
> 1 teaspoon kosher salt or coarse sea salt
> Squirt of sriracha or other Asian chile sauce, optional

1. COMBINE the carrots and daikon in a large bowl. Stir together in a small bowl the vinegar, sugar, salt, and, if you like, the sriracha, and pour over the vegetables.

2. REFRIGERATE the relish for at least 1 hour, until the carrot and daikon matchsticks bend easily. Use a slotted spoon to serve the relish on top of beef. Covered and refrigerated, the relish will keep for about 5 days.

VARIATION: Feel free to add (or even subtract) vegetables to the relish, perhaps half of a cucumber, grated, some minced red onion, or a scattering of cilantro leaves.

RUSTIC BREAD AND BASIL SALAD

A bread salad served over slices of lightly smoked prime rib or a shared hunky porterhouse soaks up the splendid juices. As fits the casualness of the recipe, feel free to bolster the salad with some small summer tomatoes or other herbs such as chives. MAKES ABOUT 4 CUPS

1/4 cup extra-virgin olive oil, or more to taste

2 garlic cloves, halved

12 ounces farm bread or other rustic bread, torn into 1-inch pieces

1/2 cup packed fresh basil leaves, with larger than bite-size pieces torn

About 1 cup tiny salad greens

About 2 tablespoons red wine vinegar

Kosher salt or coarse sea salt to taste

1. WARM the oil and garlic cloves in a large, heavy skillet over medium heat. When the garlic has colored, after about 5 minutes, remove it with a slotted spoon and discard it. Add the bread pieces, toss them with the oil, and cook until crisp and golden, about 5 minutes. This can be done up to an hour before you plan to serve the salad.

2. JUST BEFORE you are ready to serve your chosen beef dish with the salad, toss the bread croutons together in a large bowl with the remaining ingredients and a bit more oil if you wish. Spoon over the meat and enjoy right away.

BACON JAM

FOR GRILLED DISHES

Bacon jam is magnificent topping a burger or spread over some sliced tri-tip. Heck, you could probably pour it over a boulder and make it taste palatable. Feel free to try it on other types of food, too—perhaps grilled sweet potatoes or asparagus, or simple grilled bread slices. The uncooked bacon will be easier to chop when it is just out of the refrigerator. We think the jam works best on grilled rather than smoked foods. **MAKES ABOUT 2 CUPS**

1 pound sliced bacon, preferably something pretty smoky, such as Nueske's, chopped

1 large yellow onion, minced

2 garlic cloves, minced

1/4 cup plus 2 tablespoons cider vinegar

1/2 cup brewed coffee

1/2 cup packed dark brown sugar

3 tablespoons pure maple syrup or agave nectar

1 bay leaf or 1 teaspoon minced fresh thyme

1. FRY the bacon in a large, heavy skillet over medium heat, stirring occasionally. When the bacon is brown and crisp, after about 15 minutes, remove it with a slotted spoon, drain on paper towels, and reserve.

2. POUR off and set aside for another use all but 2 tablespoons of the bacon fat and stir the onion into the fat that remains in the skillet. Continue cooking over medium heat until the onion is soft and translucent, about 7 minutes more. Stir in the garlic and cook for 1 more minute.

3. POUR in the vinegar and scrape up the mixture from the bottom of the skillet. Add the coffee, brown sugar, maple syrup, bay leaf, and reserved bacon. Stir well. Turn the heat down to low, cover, and simmer for about 1 hour, stirring occasionally, until very thick and jammy. Remove the bay leaf. We like the texture as is, but if you wish, you can puree about half of the jam in a food processor and then stir it back in.

4. USE warm, or store in a covered container in the refrigerator for up to 10 days and reheat as needed. Dollop it on dinner as you would with any jam.

CORNICHON RELISH

Cornichons are those tiny French-style pickles served with pâtés and meat dishes. The bright tang of the pickles in this relish cuts the richness of a burger or even a simple top-quality steak or tenderloin. A little dab will do you. **MAKES ABOUT 3/4 CUP**

> 1/3 cup finely chopped cornichons
> 1/3 cup minced fresh flat-leaf parsley
> 2 tablespoons small capers
> 2 tablespoons extra-virgin olive oil
> 1 teaspoon red wine vinegar

1. STIR together all of the ingredients in a small bowl. Let the relish sit for 15 to 30 minutes for the flavors to meld.

2. SERVE at room temperature spooned over beef. Leftovers can be refrigerated in a covered container for another day or two.

> **VARIATION:** If you want more of a salad than a relish, increase the parsley to 1 cup or so.

PICKLED MUSTARD SEEDS

FOR TRADITIONAL BARBECUE, CONTEMPORARY SMOKED FOOD, & GRILLED DISHES

We love the little crunch and spurt of pickled mustard seeds. The hot vinegar bath that pickles the seeds also helps release their pectin, making the liquid cling to them when served over a grilled flat-iron or hanger steak, or over pastrami-cured and smoked brisket. The seeds can also be pretty darned good with a grilled piece of halibut or swordfish. MAKES ABOUT 2 CUPS

3/4 cup yellow mustard seeds

1 cup white vinegar

1/2 cup water

1/4 cup granulated sugar

1 teaspoon kosher salt or coarse sea salt

1/4 teaspoon crushed hot red chile flakes

1. DUMP the mustard seeds into a small heatproof bowl. Combine the remaining ingredients in a small saucepan and bring to a full, rolling boil over high heat. Pour the liquid over the mustard seeds and let stand for at least 3 hours.

2. SPOON a couple of teaspoons of the pickled seeds over each serving of meat. Refrigerated in a covered container, the seeds keep for up to a month.

VARIATION: For Curried Mustard Seeds, add 1/2 teaspoon curry powder to the pickling liquid before bringing it to a boil.

FABULOUS FLAVORINGS FOR CHICKEN, TURKEY, GAME BIRDS, AND OTHER POULTRY

DRY RUBS, PASTES, AND MARINADES

BARBECUED GAME BIRD SPICE

The amount of sugar in this rub indicates that it's intended for smoking rather than grilling. We use some Asian five-spice powder in it for its warm notes of star anise and cinnamon, but the overall taste profile is really woodsy American. Rub it all over quail, pheasant, dove, or duck. MAKES ABOUT 1 CUP

> 1/4 cup packed brown sugar
> 3 tablespoons freshly ground black pepper
> 2 tablespoons crushed pink peppercorns
> 2 tablespoons crumbled dried marjoram
> 2 tablespoons five-spice powder
> 2 tablespoons granulated garlic
> 2 tablespoons kosher salt or coarse sea salt

1. MIX all of the ingredients well in a small bowl. Sprinkle the rub generously on game birds, massaging it over and under the skin. Allow the seasoned game birds to sit for about 30 minutes at room temperature prior to cooking.

2. STORE any remaining rub in a covered container in a cool, dark pantry for up to several months.

CLUCKIN' CLASSIC RUB

FOR TRADITIONAL BARBECUE, CONTEMPORARY SMOKED FOOD, & GRILLED DISHES

Dry rubs and pastes are particularly good for poultry because they can flavor both the skin and the meat under it. Always take the time to rub under as well as over the skin and in both cavities, and your grilled or barbecued chicken will taste better than the fare at most restaurants. For a sauce that pairs superbly with this rub, opt for Bacon and Maple Barbecue Sauce (page 146) or Rustic Lemon Sauce (page 151). **MAKES ABOUT 3/4 CUP**

1/4 cup kosher salt or coarse sea salt
2 tablespoons garlic salt
2 tablespoons dried mustard powder
2 tablespoons crumbled dried thyme
2 tablespoons dried lemon zest
2 tablespoons freshly ground black pepper
2 teaspoons ground cayenne

1. MIX all of the ingredients well in a small bowl. Sprinkle the rub generously on chicken, massaging it over and under the skin. Allow the seasoned poultry to sit for at least 30 minutes at room temperature, or up to 8 hours wrapped or covered in the refrigerator, prior to cooking.

2. STORE any remaining rub in a covered container in a cool, dark pantry for up to several months.

spicing **TIP** Loosen up. One of the best tips we can give you for flavoring skin-on poultry is to take the time to loosen the skin so that your chosen flavoring can go both over and under the skin. Look for a loose edge and then carefully wriggle a finger, or several, in and then back and forth to pull more skin away from the meat of the poultry. If you are working with individual pieces of chicken, leave the skin attached at an edge or two so that it doesn't pull completely free. For a whole chicken, also rub the seasoning inside the bird's cavities, into all the nooks.

TARRAGON RUB

FOR GRILLED DISHES

Which came first, the chicken or the tarragon? They are simply sensational together, at least for grilling (the herbal taste gets a bit lost in a heavy dose of smoke). Don't overdo tarragon in any preparation, though, or your food will taste like grass. Use 2 to 3 tablespoons of this rub on a 3-pound chicken or 3 pounds of bone-in, skin-on chicken parts. Baste while cooking with Smoked Bacon Butter (page 144) or serve the chicken over greens with Warm Duck Fat Vinaigrette (page 158). MAKES ABOUT 1/2 CUP

1/4 cup plus 1 tablespoon dried tarragon

1 tablespoon onion powder

1 tablespoon kosher salt or coarse sea salt

1 teaspoon celery salt

1 teaspoon ground white pepper

1. MIX all of the ingredients well in a small bowl. Sprinkle the rub generously on chicken, massaging it over and under the skin. Allow the seasoned poultry to sit for about 30 minutes at room temperature prior to cooking.

2. STORE any leftovers in a covered container in a cool, dark pantry for up to several months.

CRAZY FOR CANELA RUB

FOR CONTEMPORARY SMOKED FOOD & GRILLED DISHES

Mexican cinnamon, or canela, is a bit different from the most commonly available cinnamon, which is known in the spice world as Ceylon cinnamon. The difference is not so overpowering that you can't make this rub from either type of cinnamon, but the warmth and fragrance of true canela makes it worthwhile to seek out. Use the rub on chicken, quail, or duck, and consider pairing it with Tangy Orange Baste (page 139). MAKES ABOUT 1 CUP

1/4 cup ground dried ancho chile

1/4 cup sweet paprika

2 tablespoons plus 2 teaspoons ground cinnamon, preferably canela

2 tablespoons kosher salt or coarse sea salt

1 tablespoon plus 1 teaspoon crumbled dried Mexican oregano or marjoram

1 tablespoon plus 1 teaspoon freshly ground black pepper

3/4 teaspoon ground allspice

3/4 teaspoon ground cloves

1. MIX all of the ingredients in a small bowl. Sprinkle the rub generously on poultry, massaging it over and under the skin. Allow the seasoned poultry to sit for at least 30 minutes at room temperature, or up to a few hours wrapped or covered in the refrigerator, prior to cooking.

2. STORE any remaining rub in a covered container in a cool, dark pantry for up to 3 months.

DRY BRINE FOR TURKEY

A dry brine differs from a rub essentially in the prominence of the salt in it. It works best on a whole turkey or a turkey breast because the amount of salt will not overpower the thick meat. If you're a serious fan of garlic, add a minced fresh clove or two to the mixture. Just as with a dry rub, the brine mixture should be massaged both under and over the skin as well as inside the turkey. The seasoned bird will taste best if it can sit in the refrigerator for at least 8 hours or up to a full day before proceeding. This recipe makes enough for a 12- to 15-pound turkey. If you're smoking the turkey, either Crafty Beer Mop (page 140) or Smoked Bacon Butter (page 144) would make a great baste. MAKES ABOUT 3/4 CUP

1/4 cup plus 2 tablespoons kosher salt or coarse sea salt

3 tablespoons freshly grated lemon zest

2 tablespoons coarsely ground black pepper

1 tablespoon lightly crushed pink peppercorns

1 tablespoon garlic powder

2 teaspoons crumbled dried sage or crumbled dried thyme

1. **MIX** all of the ingredients thoroughly in a bowl. Sprinkle the rub generously on turkey, massaging it over and under the skin. Allow the seasoned turkey to sit for 8 to 24 hours wrapped or covered in the refrigerator. Rinse the brine off the turkey, and pat the meat dry with paper towels before cooking.

2. **STORE** any leftovers in a covered container in a cool, dark pantry for up to 1 month.

spicing **TIP** We are not big fans of brining, especially with water-filled mixtures. To our minds, it simply waters down the meat by plumping it up, and makes good meat or poultry take other flavors too completely. We'd rather have a turkey, for instance, that tastes like a turkey, and not like maple syrup or other popular brining flavors.

HERBES DE LUBERON RUB

FOR CONTEMPORARY SMOKED FOOD & GRILLED DISHES

France's Luberon region, an area of rugged hills, rises east of Avignon in Provence. We designed this rub with richly flavored duck or goose in mind. You can use the blend on a whole chicken or chicken parts, too, but use a slightly lighter hand for the lighter poultry. Most French herb blends have no salt, but we've included it here since it is common in rubs for outdoor cooking. Be sure to use culinary lavender rather than the flower buds of just any garden lavender to avoid a big hit of camphor. Buy it from a spice store if you are uncertain. With the addition of a tablespoon of dried rosemary, this rub is equally smashing on any lamb destined for the grill. MAKES ABOUT 1 CUP

> $1/2$ cup dried basil
> 2 tablespoons dried marjoram
> $1^1/2$ tablespoons dried lavender flowers
> $1^1/2$ tablespoons coarsely ground fennel seeds
> 2 teaspoons kosher salt or coarse sea salt

1. STIR together all of the ingredients in a small bowl. Sprinkle the rub generously on duck or goose and more lightly on chicken, massaging it over and under the skin. Allow the seasoned poultry to sit for at least 30 minutes at room temperature, or up to 8 hours wrapped or covered in the refrigerator, prior to cooking.

2. STORE any leftovers in a covered container in a cool, dark pantry for up to 6 months.

VARIATION: If you like to marinate chicken with a slightly sweet liquid, mix a batch of this dry rub with 1 cup dry white wine, 2 tablespoons honey, and 2 tablespoons extra-virgin olive oil. Marinate up to overnight, wrapped or covered in the refrigerator, prior to cooking.

FIERY GINGER PASTE

We like the heavier spice notes of this Chinese-inspired paste when working with duck or other dark-meat birds. It also pairs better with heavier smoke than Kung Pow for Chicken (page 124) on all poultry, chicken included. The paste is best put together for one meal at a time. MAKES ABOUT 1/2 CUP

2 tablespoons frozen orange juice concentrate, thawed

2 tablespoons soy sauce

2 tablespoons minced or grated fresh ginger

1 teaspoon five-spice powder

1 teaspoon ground cinnamon

1 teaspoon ground dried hot red chile, such as cayenne, or more to taste

1/2 teaspoon ground Szechuan peppercorns

1. STIR together all of the ingredients in a small bowl. Use the mixture within a few hours for the best flavor.

2. RUB the paste generously on poultry, massaging it over and under the skin. Allow the seasoned poultry to sit for about 30 minutes at room temperature prior to cooking.

spicing **TIP** **Frozen orange juice concentrate sometimes makes a better seasoning ingredient than fresh orange juice, because it offers bolder taste and less liquid. Used in judicious amounts, it can help form a deeply colored crust. We try to find small cans of it, then partially thaw them, just enough to be able to chunk out the amount that we need, and return the rest to the freezer. The metal lids for these paperboard cans usually fit back snugly on top to keep out air.**

KUNG POW FOR CHICKEN

FOR GRILLED DISHES

This seasoning paste incorporates the zingy flavors of kung pao chicken. We use peanut oil to mimic the peanuts generally used in the stir-fry preparation, but you can opt for a neutral vegetable oil if you wish. You can also adjust the amount of chile pow in the dish for your level of tolerance. This one's best made up for one meal at a time, so the amount's perfect for one plump chicken, whole or in parts. **MAKES ABOUT 1/2 CUP**

> 1 tablespoon peanut oil or vegetable oil
>
> 1 tablespoon soy sauce
>
> 2 teaspoons minced or grated fresh ginger
>
> 2 teaspoons Chinese rice wine or dry sherry
>
> 2 teaspoons hoisin sauce
>
> 2 garlic cloves, minced
>
> 1 teaspoon Asian sesame oil
>
> 1 teaspoon ground dried hot red chile, such as cayenne, or more to taste

1. STIR together all of the ingredients in a small bowl. Use the mixture within a few hours for the best flavor.

2. RUB the paste generously on poultry, massaging it over and under the skin. Allow the seasoned poultry to sit for about 30 minutes at room temperature prior to cooking.

spicing **TIP** When making up your own idea for pastes, choose an ingredient or two that will allow the mixture to cling to the surface of foods. Here, sticky hoisin sauce is one of those ingredients, and the ginger helps give body to the paste, too. Citrus zest, minced onion, and mustard are other ingredients with clinging power.

JERK PASTE

This culinary all-star from Jamaica has become so popular in recent decades that every outdoor cook should have a signature jerk seasoning, preferably homemade. This paste makes enough for several chickens or their parts or perhaps a dozen quail. (It is almost equally good on pork.) To further perfume the poultry—and have the best-smelling backyard in the neighborhood—toss some cinnamon sticks, whole allspice, and soaked bay leaves into your fire. You probably know this already, but handle the incendiary Scotch bonnet chiles with care, wearing gloves when you cut and seed them. MAKES ABOUT 1¼ CUPS

1 small bunch scallions, both white and green parts, roughly chopped
Walnut-sized chunk of fresh ginger
3 tablespoons vegetable oil
1 or 2 fresh Scotch bonnet or habanero chiles, seeded
1 tablespoon packed brown sugar
1 tablespoon fresh thyme leaves
1 tablespoon freshly ground allspice
1 tablespoon dried onion flakes or granulated onion or 2 teaspoons onion powder
1 tablespoon kosher salt or coarse sea salt
1 teaspoon freshly grated nutmeg
½ teaspoon ground cinnamon

1. COMBINE all of the ingredients in a food processor and process until a paste forms. Don't stand directly over the processor because the chile fumes pack a mighty wallop. Use the paste right away or refrigerate in a covered container for up to several weeks.

2. RUB the paste generously on poultry, massaging it over and under the skin. Allow the seasoned poultry to sit for at least 30 minutes at room temperature, or up to 8 hours wrapped or covered in the refrigerator, prior to cooking.

VARIATION: To make a jerk vinaigrette to serve as a table sauce, reserve 2 tablespoons of the jerk paste. Mix the paste into about $^1/_2$ cup vegetable or sunflower oil, 3 tablespoons white vinegar, and a pinch or two each brown sugar and salt.

spicing **TIP** **Cooking with wood contributes fragrance and flavor to foods, especially to slow-cooked items that have plenty of time to soak up the smoke. You can also add subtle but distinct layers of other flavors by putting aromatic spices or seasonings in the fire. In addition to cinnamon sticks, allspice berries, and soaked bay leaves, experiment with whole nutmegs, cracked whole nuts or nut shells, star anise, juniper berries, peppercorns, coffee beans, tea leaves, or orange or other citrus peels. If you have loads of grapevine cuttings, rosemary branches, or sage sprigs in your garden, by all means consider using them. However, if you need to buy items like these, or other fresh herbs, we think it's more flavorful and cost-effective to put the flavoring agent in the dish instead of the fire.**

PEPITA AND CUMIN PASTE

FOR GRILLED DISHES

Try this on quail or duck to give it a touch of Mexican flavor without chile heat. Shelled pumpkin seeds, known commonly in the Southwest and other Hispanic areas as pepitas, make a good mild base for a seasoning paste. They can be found in many supermarkets today, usually in the vicinity of shelled nuts. Pumpkin seed oil will further enhance the sweet earthy quality of the pepitas, but olive oil is fine to use here, too. The delicacy of the paste makes it best for grilled items. You might want to pair chicken flavored with this paste with the finishing sauce Quick Black Mole (page 156).

MAKES ABOUT 3/4 CUP

4 garlic cloves, peeled

1/2 cup pepitas (shelled pumpkin seeds)

2 tablespoons fresh marjoram leaves, preferably, or fresh parsley leaves

1 tablespoon pumpkin seed oil or extra-virgin olive oil

2 teaspoons ground cumin

2 teaspoons kosher salt or coarse sea salt

1. PLACE the garlic cloves in a small, heavy skillet. Over medium-low heat, toast the cloves until softened and lightly colored, 6 to 8 minutes.

2. DROP the garlic cloves into a running food processor and mince them. Stop the processor, put in the pepitas and marjoram, and process until finely chopped. With the processor still running, add in the oil. Add the cumin and salt and pulse an extra time or two to incorporate them.

3. USE THE paste within one day of making it. Rub the paste generously on poultry, massaging it over and under the skin. Allow the seasoned poultry to sit for at least 30 minutes at room temperature, or up to a few hours wrapped or covered in the refrigerator, prior to cooking.

TBILISI GRAPE-WALNUT PASTE

FOR GRILLED DISHES

The American state of Georgia is known for peaches, pecans, and pork barbecue, among other things. On the other side of the world, the Republic of Georgia and its capital, Tbilisi, are also known for their food. In the Caucasus, the region at the edge of Europe and Asia, the other Georgia sits between the Caspian and Black Seas. The location makes for a feast of produce, with grapes and walnuts among the bountiful offerings. Try this paste on dark-meat poultry, such as chicken thighs or legs, duck, or pheasant. Cilantro commonly finds its way into seasonings of this sort, but its flavor gets lost when heated. Rather than adding it to the paste, scatter cilantro leaves over the finished dish. **MAKES ABOUT 3/4 CUP**

> 1/4 cup white grape juice
> 1/4 cup red wine vinegar
> 2 tablespoons walnut oil
> 2 tablespoons finely chopped walnuts
> 1 teaspoon ground dried ginger
> 1 teaspoon kosher salt or coarse sea salt

1. WHISK together all of the ingredients in a medium-size bowl. Use within a few hours for the best flavor.

2. RUB the paste generously on poultry, massaging it over and under the skin. Allow the seasoned poultry to sit for at least 30 minutes at room temperature, or up to a few hours wrapped or covered in the refrigerator, prior to cooking.

VINDALOO PASTE

FOR GRILLED DISHES

This robust and fiery Indian spice paste is reminiscent of those used in Goa, where the Portuguese colonists influenced the cooking heavily. The complexity of tastes comes through best with grilled dishes. A full-day soak in the paste provides peak flavor to bone-in or boneless chicken parts. This makes enough for about 4 pounds of poultry. Serve it with the cooling Lychee-Pineapple Salad (page 163). **MAKES ABOUT 1 CUP**

1 tablespoon coriander seeds
1 tablespoon black peppercorns
1 teaspoon cumin seeds
3 whole cloves
3 to 5 small hot fresh chiles, such as bird, cayenne, or de árbol
1 small garlic head (about 10 cloves), peeled
1/2 cup rice vinegar
Walnut-size nugget of fresh ginger
1 tablespoon packed brown sugar
1 teaspoon ground turmeric
1 teaspoon kosher salt or coarse sea salt

1. TOAST the coriander seeds, peppercorns, cumin seeds, cloves, and chiles in a small dry skillet over medium-low heat. When the spices become fragrant, dump them into a spice mill or mortar and grind until fine.

2. TRANSFER the spice mixture to a food processor. Add the remaining ingredients and process the mixture until a paste forms. Use right away or store in a covered container in the refrigerator for up to 1 month.

3. RUB the paste generously on poultry, massaging it over and under the skin. Allow the seasoned poultry to sit for at least 30 minutes at room temperature, or up to a few hours wrapped or covered in the refrigerator, prior to cooking.

spicing **TIP** If you want Indian flavor accents but not the heat of vindaloo, you might opt for a yogurt paste instead. Combine 1 cup plain full-fat Greek yogurt with the zest and juice of 1 large lemon, then mix in 2 teaspoons ground coriander, 1 teaspoon salt, and 1/2 teaspoon ground cayenne. You'll end up with super-juicy and mildly spiced chicken.

CITRUS PASTE FOR POULTRY

FOR CONTEMPORARY SMOKED FOOD & GRILLED DISHES

This paste will pump up fragrance and flavor in chicken parts, a whole chicken, or four duck breasts. It's best made up fresh whenever you plan to use it. The citrus tang is especially sweet with smoked fare. **MAKES ABOUT 1/2 CUP**

2 tablespoons packed minced fresh orange zest plus 2 tablespoons fresh orange juice

2 tablespoons packed minced fresh lemon zest plus 1 teaspoon fresh lemon juice

2 teaspoons ground coriander

1 teaspoon kosher salt or coarse sea salt

1 teaspoon vegetable oil or sunflower oil

1/2 teaspoon ground white pepper

1. BUZZ all of the ingredients in a food processor until a paste forms. Use right away. Rub the paste generously on poultry, massaging it over and under the skin.

2. ALLOW the seasoned poultry to sit for about 30 minutes at room temperature prior to cooking.

VARIATION: Turn this paste into a marinade by adding 1 1/2 cups freshly squeezed grapefruit juice (from about 3 grapefruit). All winter long, we have hefty Rio Star grapefruits delivered to our door from McAllen, Texas, in the heart of the Rio Grande Valley's citrus region. You can use other grapefruit, but they won't have the complex juice of a Rio Star.

DIRTY VODKA MARTINI MARINADE

Guests love chicken bathed in a martini marinade. If you are using it for grilling, don't mix a hot, flaming fire with any marinade fueled like this with alcohol. Make sure to pat the surfaces of the chicken dry with paper towels before placing it over the fire, which should be kept at a medium heat level, enough to cook chicken through without burning the surface. MAKES ABOUT 2 CUPS

> 3/4 cup brine from a jar of green olives
> 3/4 cup vodka
> 1/4 cup dry vermouth
> 1/4 cup water
> 1 tablespoon olive oil

1. MIX all of the ingredients in a bowl or in a large zipper-lock plastic bag. Use within a few hours for the best flavor.

2. POUR the marinade over poultry, massaging it over and under the skin. Allow the seasoned poultry to sit for at least 30 minutes at room temperature, or up to a few hours wrapped or covered in the refrigerator, prior to cooking.

VARIATIONS: To make a Bloody Mary-nade instead, leave out the vermouth and substitute 1/2 cup tomato juice and a few splashes of hot sauce. Or, for a strange-sounding concoction we call Weird Green Marinade, leave out the vodka and vermouth and replace them with dill pickle juice. If you like, add up to 1 tablespoon green Tabasco sauce. Remarkably good.

CURRIED COCONUT MILK MARINADE

FOR GRILLED DISHES

We find this marinade nice for chicken breasts and perfect for chicken satay. If you want to baste while grilling, set aside one-third of the marinade and mix it with an equal amount of pineapple juice. For extra verve, serve the chicken with Indonesian Peanut Sauce (page 152). MAKES ABOUT 2 CUPS

14- to 15-ounce can unsweetened coconut milk

2 tablespoons chopped tender lemongrass, bruised with the side of a chef's knife to release more flavor

2 tablespoons palm sugar (see Spicing Tip) or packed brown sugar

2 shallots, minced

2 teaspoons curry powder

1 1/2 teaspoons kosher salt or coarse sea salt

1. MIX all of the ingredients in a bowl or in a large zipper-lock plastic bag. Use within a few hours for the best flavor.

2. POUR the marinade over poultry, massaging it over and under the skin. Allow the seasoned poultry to sit for at least 30 minutes at room temperature, or up to a few hours wrapped or covered in the refrigerator, prior to cooking.

spicing **TIP** Palm sugar, used traditionally in a variety of tropical cuisines, comes from the sap of a sugar or date palm. It is unrefined, so it has toasty, almost caramelized, undertones. Find it in hard little tan to brown cakes, or in a jar, at Latin American or Indian markets or from online sources. It will soften in the coconut milk.

CRANBERRY-ORANGE HOLIDAY MARINADE

FOR TRADITIONAL BARBECUE & CONTEMPORARY SMOKED FOOD

A fruity soak for a turkey or a pair of pheasants, this may elevate the joy of a holiday meal. MAKES ABOUT 1 GALLON

1 gallon sweetened cranberry or cran-apple juice

3-ounce can frozen orange juice concentrate, thawed

1 large onion, chopped

2 tablespoons crumbled dried sage

2 tablespoons kosher salt or coarse sea salt

1. MIX all of the ingredients in a large bowl. Use within a few hours for the best flavor.

2. POUR the marinade over the poultry and let sit for at least 30 minutes at room temperature, or up to a few hours wrapped or covered in the refrigerator, prior to cooking.

spicing TIP Want a quick and dirty marinade for chicken? Simply use a salty Asian fish sauce on chicken or chicken parts, both over and under the skin. We particularly like Red Boat brand. If you want to appear more energetic, toss in a little ground black pepper.

GINGER ALE AND GARLIC MARINADE

FOR TRADITIONAL BARBECUE, CONTEMPORARY SMOKED FOOD, & GRILLED DISHES

Chicken, game hens, quail, and pheasant drink this up. Deepen the complexity if you wish by using a real ginger beer rather than the more common soft drink. **MAKES ABOUT 1½ CUPS**

> 12-ounce bottle or can ginger ale
> 1 tablespoon minced or grated fresh ginger
> 1 tablespoon vegetable oil or sunflower oil
> 1½ teaspoons kosher salt or coarse sea salt

1. **MIX** all of the ingredients in a bowl. Use within a few hours or refrigerate in a covered container and use within the next few days.

2. **POUR** the marinade over the poultry and let sit for at least 30 minutes at room temperature, or up to 8 hours wrapped or covered in the refrigerator, prior to cooking.

spicing **TIP** You may notice that we vary the times in which we suggest that poultry should soak in its flavoring prior to cooking. When using seasonings with more acid, such as vinegar or citrus juice, we suggest shorter times, because the acid can make the poultry soft and flabby if it is marinated too long.

MARSALA-BALSAMIC MARINADE

FOR GRILLED DISHES

A dry Marsala is Italy's favorite brandy-fortified wine. Like other fortified wines, it has a much longer shelf life than regular wine after it's opened, so you can make other batches of this marinade from the same bottle. The flavors go great with guinea hen, game hen, chicken thighs, or simple chicken sausages. **MAKES ABOUT 1¼ CUPS**

3/4 cup dry Marsala wine

1/4 cup plus 2 tablespoons inexpensive balsamic vinegar

3 tablespoons olive oil

1 or 2 salt-cured anchovies, filleted and mashed, or 1 teaspoon kosher salt
or coarse sea salt

1 garlic clove, minced

1. MIX all of the ingredients in a small bowl. Use within a few hours for the best flavor.

2. POUR the marinade over the poultry and let sit for at least 30 minutes at room temperature, or up to a few hours wrapped or covered in the refrigerator, prior to cooking.

spicing **TIP** Hands down, the most popular marinade for chicken parts cooked in the great outdoors has got to be Italian salad dressing, the kind no one uses in Italy. The bottled American-made condiment, which both of us loved as children, can still work. However, if you want fresher flavors, make your own with extra-virgin olive oil, fresh lemon juice, a minced garlic clove or two, some freshly grated Parmesan or Romano, and minced fresh parsley, to your taste.

PERUVIAN MARINADE

FOR GRILLED DISHES

Peruvian grilled chicken bursts with piquancy and soy tang, the latter a result of Asian immigration to the country. Pour this marinade over chicken parts or a full "spatchcocked" bird, one that has had its backbone cut out and then is pressed flat so it can be cooked over a direct, rather than indirect, grill fire. Ají amarillo, a yellow-orange chile used widely in Peruvian cuisine, adds a wonderful nuance to this marinade. MAKES ABOUT 1¼ CUPS

> 1/2 cup freshly squeezed lime juice
>
> 1/4 cup soy sauce
>
> 1/4 cup chicken stock, preferably a reduced-sodium variety
>
> 1/4 cup olive oil
>
> 3 or 4 garlic cloves, minced
>
> 1 teaspoon crushed or ground dried ají amarillo chile or ají amarillo chile paste (see Spicing Tip) or 1/2 teaspoon ground dried ancho chile plus 1/4 teaspoon ground dried habanero chile, or more to taste

1. **MIX** all of the ingredients in a small bowl. Use within a few hours for the best flavor.

2. **POUR** the marinade over the poultry and let sit for at least 30 minutes at room temperature, or up to a few hours wrapped or covered in the refrigerator, prior to cooking.

spicing TIP **Ají amarillo is still somewhat challenging to find in many areas of the country, but it can be bought whole or ground from savory spiceshop.com or penderys.com, and in a variety of chile paste forms from amazon.com. Because the products vary in heat, we suggest you try a bit on a cracker or cucumber before committing yourself to an amount in the marinade.**

MOPS AND BASTES

TANGY ORANGE BASTE

FOR GRILLED DISHES

This light baste is meant specifically for grilled food, so you don't need a big batch for long basting. For a full measure of citrus tang, use this on poultry first flavored with Citrus Paste for Poultry (page 131). **MAKES ABOUT 1½ CUPS**

> 1 cup fresh orange juice (from about 3 large oranges)
> 3 tablespoons fresh lime juice
> 2 garlic cloves, minced
> 2 tablespoons unsalted butter
> 1 teaspoon kosher salt or coarse sea salt

1. COMBINE all of the ingredients in a saucepan.

2. HEAT the baste before you plan to use it initially and keep it warm over low heat between applications. Brush it on the poultry once or twice early in the grilling process.

CRAFTY BEER MOP

FOR TRADITIONAL BARBECUE & CONTEMPORARY SMOKED FOOD

Beer bears repeating in different forms as the base for a barbecue and grilling baste because it's a core element of the American outdoor cooking tradition. The one thing that's changed notably over the years that we've dealt with this subject is the range of full-bodied, truly tasty craft beers that now abound. Kick up your game by using a chocolate porter or oatmeal stout, or an otherwise interesting flavor. You will really be able to taste the difference on mild-mannered poultry. Use this mop if you are barbecuing chicken massaged in Cluckin' Classic Rub (page 117). **MAKES ABOUT 3 CUPS**

12-ounce bottle or can craft beer

3/4 cup water

1/2 cup cider vinegar

2 tablespoons sunflower or vegetable oil

1 tablespoon dry rub used to flavor the food, optional, or 1 teaspoon kosher salt or coarse sea salt

1. **COMBINE** all of the ingredients in a saucepan.

2. **HEAT** the mop before you plan to use it initially and keep it warm over low heat between bastes. Apply to the poultry about once an hour.

spicing **TIP** If you omit the water and oil from this mop, you have the makings of a great version of beer-can chicken, also known as chicken on a throne. You'll want to use a can, rather than a bottle of beer, and open the top fully with a can opener rather than the little pull tab. Take a few sips from the can (cook's treat) before adding the vinegar and dry rub to the can. Then set a nice plump chicken onto the can, place on the barbecue grate, and smoke away.

CIDER SPLASH

FOR TRADITIONAL BARBECUE, CONTEMPORARY SMOKED FOOD, & GRILLED DISHES

This works wonderfully on pheasant, quail, or game hens. If you have a choice, opt for a tangier rather than a sweeter cider, which adds more dimensions in flavor. Brush or drizzle this on food cooking on the grill or smoker. Because of the shorter cooking time needed for grilled poultry, you can likely get by with just half a batch of the splash. For a good table condiment with this, try Chunky Cinnamon Applesauce (page 166). **MAKES ABOUT 3 CUPS**

2 cups apple cider or juice

3/4 cup water

1 tablespoon sunflower or vegetable oil

1 tablespoon Dijon mustard

1 tablespoon dry rub used to flavor the food, optional, or 1 teaspoon kosher salt or coarse sea salt

1. COMBINE all of the ingredients in a saucepan.

2. HEAT the mop before you plan to use it initially and keep it warm over low heat between bastes. Apply to the poultry one or two times when you are grilling it or about once an hour when you are smoking it.

VARIATION: For a sweeter splash, substitute white grape juice for half of the cider.

spicing **TIP** Mops are traditional for smoke cooking but not for grilling. However, using a mop or baste on grilled poultry can build up layers of flavor while the bird cooks. Just forgo the mop in the last few minutes of grilling so that the surface of the poultry has a chance to crisp up a bit before coming off the fire.

CHAI SPLASH

We've made our own tea bastes in the past, often using smoky Lapsang Souchong tea for tea-smoked chicken or duck in particular. Playing around with chai concentrate, we discovered it bundles flavors fast and efficiently. It's faultless on that tea-smoked duck, but just as delectable on grilled chicken breasts or thighs. Almond oil will give the baste a hint of buttery nuttiness, but if you don't have it, you can get by with a neutral vegetable oil. Chicken flavored with Crazy for Canela Rub (page 119) is one good pairing with this baste. Serve the chicken at the table with Lychee-Pineapple Salad (page 163). MAKES ABOUT 3 CUPS

> 2 cups packaged chai concentrate, such as Tazo
> About 1 cup water
> 1 tablespoon almond oil or vegetable oil

1. POUR the chai concentrate into a small saucepan. Taste the concentrate. Stir in water as needed to dilute it to a still-robust level. Stir in the oil.

2. HEAT the liquid before you plan to use it initially and keep it warm over low heat between bastes. Apply to the poultry one to two times when you are grilling it or about once an hour when you are smoking it.

SMOKED BACON BUTTER

FOR GRILLED DISHES

If you're not barbecuing something else, make this smoked butter in a stovetop smoker or other easily fired-up smoker. Bacon drippings and a bit of smoked paprika help contribute a good measure of outdoorsy character. Try the compound butter on grilled corn on the cob or fish as well as poultry.

MAKES ABOUT 1 CUP

> 8 tablespoons (1 stick) chilled unsalted butter, cut into 2-tablespoon chunks
> 1/2 cup chilled bacon drippings
> 1 or 2 teaspoons soy sauce or a light sprinkling of kosher salt or coarse sea salt
> 1 teaspoon smoked Spanish paprika

1. PREPARE your smoker for barbecuing, bringing the temperature to 180°F to 220°F. If you are using a stovetop smoker, the butter will cook at a higher heat, so reduce the cooking time.

2. PLACE the butter and bacon drippings in a smoke-proof shallow dish. Shake the soy sauce over and sprinkle with the paprika. Place the dish in the smoker, as far away from the heat as possible. Cook until melted, about 15 minutes.

3. USE AS is, or chill the butter until it begins to firm. Form it into a log, cover, and refrigerate for up to 3 days. It will keep for another week, but gradually the smokiness fades. Slather on grilled foods once or twice as they cook.

spicing **TIP** We suggest unsalted butter in many recipes, even ones that we add salt to—in the form of soy sauce in this case. Different brands of salted butters can vary a good bit in their sodium level. Using the precise amount of salt you like gives you control over the result. Salt acts as a preservative, so salted butter keeps longer, but it doesn't necessarily keep its sweet, fresh flavor throughout its shelf life. To extend the life of unsalted butter, you can freeze it for up to several weeks.

YAKITORI GLAZE

FOR GRILLED DISHES

Traditionally brushed on small skewers loaded with bits of dark-meat chicken, this Japanese classic is good with duck or dark turkey meat, too. It also works well on boneless chicken breasts. When using a painted-on glaze like this, you don't need any other seasoning before or after cooking.

MAKES ABOUT 1½ CUPS

8 ounces chicken necks, wings, or a combination
1 cup mirin
1 cup dry sake
1 cup soy sauce
Walnut-size chunk of fresh ginger, thinly sliced
2 garlic cloves, thinly sliced
2 tablespoons packed brown sugar
1 teaspoon freshly ground black pepper

1. CHOP the chicken parts with a cleaver into 1-inch pieces. Place in the bottom of a heavy saucepan. Place the pan over medium-high heat and cover to sweat the chicken parts for 5 minutes. Uncover, stir, and continue cooking until the chicken is medium-brown, a few more minutes.

2. POUR in the mirin, scraping up the browned mixture from the bottom. Stir in the remaining ingredients. Reduce the heat so that occasional bubbles burst on the surface. Reduce the mixture by half, about 30 minutes, stirring occasionally. Strain the glaze, discarding the solids.

3. USE THE glaze warm, brushed onto poultry in the last few minutes of cooking. It can be refrigerated in a covered container for up to 1 week.

BACON AND MAPLE BARBECUE SAUCE

FOR TRADITIONAL BARBECUE, CONTEMPORARY SMOKED FOOD, & GRILLED DISHES

Bacon and maple are the operative flavors here, but it's the undertones of vanilla extract and bourbon that make this sauce far from ordinary. It's a fine finish for "barbecued" chicken, whether cooked by smoke or over a grill fire.

MAKES ABOUT 1¼ CUPS

3 tablespoons bacon drippings

1 small onion, minced

1/3 cup pure maple syrup

1/3 cup Dijon mustard

1/4 cup water

2 tablespoons ketchup

2 tablespoons bourbon or other whiskey

1 tablespoon Worcestershire sauce

1/4 teaspoon pure vanilla extract

1. WARM the bacon drippings in a large saucepan over medium heat. Stir in the onion and cook until softened and lightly colored, about 7 minutes. Stir in the remaining ingredients and bring to a boil. Reduce the heat to a bare simmer and cook until the flavors have melded and the sauce has thickened, about 20 minutes.

2. SERVE warm or at room temperature on or alongside poultry. Stored in a covered container in the refrigerator, the sauce will keep for about 2 weeks.

STRAWBERRY-BALSAMIC SAUCE

FOR GRILLED DISHES

In Italy, strawberries are traditionally drizzled with a few precious drops of high-quality balsamic as a finishing flourish at the table. That was the *gustoso* inspiration for this *gustoso* blend. Try it brushed on boneless, skinless chicken breasts (the ultimate blank canvas) in the last few minutes of cooking, and save some for a table sauce. **MAKES ABOUT 1½ CUPS**

> 1 tablespoon olive oil
> 1 tablespoon lard or more olive oil
> 2 garlic cloves, minced
> 1 cup inexpensive balsamic vinegar
> 1 cup duck stock or chicken stock
> ½ cup strawberry jam or jelly
> Kosher salt or coarse sea salt
> Freshly ground black pepper

1. WARM the oil and lard in a medium-size saucepan over medium heat. Add the garlic and sauté for 1 minute. Pour in the balsamic vinegar, stock, and jam. Bring the mixture to a boil. Reduce the heat to a low simmer and reduce the sauce by about half, about 15 minutes. Season with salt and pepper to taste and remove from the heat.

2. USE THE sauce as a baste on grilled poultry, if you wish, and also serve it warm on or alongside the food. Refrigerate leftovers in a covered container for up to a week, but reheat it before serving again.

> VARIATION: To make a pomegranate sauce, good for quail, chicken, or duck, cut the quantity of balsamic vinegar to ¼ cup and add 2 cups pomegranate juice. If the juice comes from fresh pomegranates, save a handful of the jewel-like seeds to scatter over the completed dish. If you come across pomegranate jam or jelly, switch out the strawberry jam or jelly for it.

NORTHERN ALABAMA WHITE LIGHTNING

This sauce is in the style of **Big Bob Gibson's** in Decatur, Alabama, and other bastions of barbecued chicken in northern Alabama. **MAKES ABOUT 3 CUPS**

2 cups mayonnaise

1 cup white vinegar

2 teaspoons Worcestershire sauce

2 garlic cloves, minced

1 tablespoon freshly ground black pepper

2 teaspoons kosher salt or coarse sea salt

1/2 to 1 teaspoon ground cayenne

1. WHISK together all of the ingredients in a medium-size bowl.

2. SERVE the sauce warm or chilled with poultry. Refrigerate any remaining sauce in a covered container for up to 3 weeks.

VARIATION: The sauce can be used as the basis of a White Lightning Mop, too. Double the quantity of vinegar in that case and add a little water to thin the mixture. Heat the mop before you plan to use it initially and keep it warm over low heat between bastes.

SAUCE DIABLE

Generally considered the world's greatest culinary encyclopedia, the *Larousse Gastronomique*, focused fully on French cuisine, was published in 1938 and first translated into English in 1961. Author Prosper Montagné included several versions of this *sauce à la diable* for grilled chicken. The sauce does not seem so devilish today, when fiery chiles like *bhut jolokia* and Scotch bonnet fuel some high-octane seasonings, but the old idea still results in a beautifully balanced and richly flavorful mixture. It's best used immediately after preparation. You need only a couple of tablespoons per serving of chicken.

MAKES ABOUT 1 CUP

1 cup dry white wine

1 tablespoon white wine vinegar

1 tablespoon minced shallot

1/2 teaspoon crumbled dried thyme

1/2 bay leaf

2 pinches freshly ground black pepper

1/2 cup demi-glace (see Spicing Tip, page 51)

2 teaspoons Worcestershire sauce

1 tablespoon unsalted butter

2 teaspoons minced fresh parsley

1/4 teaspoon ground cayenne

1. COMBINE the wine, vinegar, shallot, thyme, bay leaf, and pepper in a small saucepan. Bring to a boil over medium-high heat and reduce the liquid by approximately half, 5 to 10 minutes. Strain the mixture, discarding the solids.

2. RETURN the liquid to the pan and stir in the demi-glace and Worcestershire sauce. Bring the mixture back just to a simmer, remove from the heat, and immediately whisk in the butter. When the butter has disappeared into the sauce, whisk in the parsley and cayenne. Serve the warm sauce on or alongside grilled chicken.

RUSTIC LEMON SAUCE

FOR TRADITIONAL BARBECUE, CONTEMPORARY SMOKED FOOD, & GRILLED DISHES

Here's a no-cook combo that packs a lot of pizzazz for chicken. Serve it on the side with a whole chicken or chicken parts. Anything flavored with Tarragon Rub (page 118) is a great match. MAKES ABOUT 1¼ CUPS

2 large lemons

1 tablespoon Dijon mustard

1 teaspoon Worcestershire sauce

1 garlic clove, minced

3/4 cup extra-virgin olive oil

1/2 teaspoon kosher salt or coarse sea salt, or more to taste

1/2 teaspoon crushed hot red chile flakes, or more to taste

1. GRATE the zest from one of the lemons. Cut off and discard the remaining white pith. Cut the fruit in half, discard the seeds, and chop the lemon into small bits. Place the lemon zest and lemon bits, along with any juice, in a bowl. Squeeze the juice from the second lemon and add the juice to the bowl.

2. WHISK in the mustard, Worcestershire sauce, and garlic. When combined, whisk in the oil and season with salt and red chile. Serve the sauce right away alongside chicken. Refrigerate leftovers in a covered container for up to 1 week, but allow the sauce to come back close to room temperature before serving again.

VARIATION: Add a fresh herb or two to the sauce. Tarragon, parsley, basil, thyme, or lovage would all be good choices.

INDONESIAN PEANUT SAUCE

FOR GRILLED DISHES

You can make an Indonesian-style satay sauce from grocery store peanut butter or even buy one ready-made. We figure, though, anyone reading this book takes real pride in their outdoor cooking and accompaniments, so we're going to make this one from scratch, with fresh-roasted peanuts. The Southeast Asian seasonings can be found in most any Asian market these days or from many online sources. Don't think this sauce is only for little skewers of chicken, though. It offers welcome verve to boneless chicken or duck breasts, or to a big casual salad made with chicken or duck, fresh greens, and leaves of fresh basil, mint, and cilantro. **MAKES ABOUT 3 CUPS**

1 cup raw shelled peanuts

1/3 cup chopped shallots

2 garlic cloves, minced

1 tablespoon chopped fresh galangal or ginger

2 to 4 fresh or dried small hot red chiles, such as bird, cayenne, or de árbol

2 tablespoons peanut oil or vegetable oil

2 kaffir lime leaves or 1 teaspoon freshly grated lime zest plus 1 teaspoon fresh lime juice

6-inch stalk of lemongrass, bruised with the side of a chef's knife

14- to 15-ounce can unsweetened coconut milk, preferably a full-fat variety

2 tablespoons tamarind paste

2 tablespoons palm sugar (see Spicing Tip, page 134) *or* packed dark brown sugar, or more to taste

2 cinnamon sticks, each about 4 inches long

2 teaspoons coriander seeds, toasted in a dry skillet and ground

1. PREHEAT the oven to 375°F. Place the peanuts on a baking sheet and bake until lightly browned and fragrant, about 5 minutes. Pour the warm nuts into a food processor. Process the nuts, using short pulses, until a coarse paste forms, about 1 minute.

2. POUND together the shallots, garlic, galangal, and chiles in a mortar.

3. WARM the oil in a medium-size sauté pan over medium heat. Stir in the pounded shallot mixture and fry, stirring a few times, until the mixture is very fragrant and a couple of shades darker in color, about 5 minutes. Mix in the kaffir lime leaves and lemongrass and warm through. Immediately stir in the coconut milk, followed by the tamarind paste, sugar, cinnamon sticks, and coriander. Simmer the sauce for 10 minutes, then mix in the peanuts and keep cooking until the flavors are melded together, another 2 or 3 minutes. Remove and discard the lime leaves, lemongrass, and cinnamon sticks. Taste and add more sugar if you wish.

4. THE SAUCE can be served warm with satay or other food or cooled to room temperature. If it thickens too much to spoon easily, thin with a tablespoon or so of warm water. The sauce can be refrigerated in a covered container and kept for up to 2 weeks. Reheat the sauce and whisk it together before serving.

SHERRY-SHALLOT SAUCE

Dry fino sherry goes well with quail and duck, as do apples and shallots. The subtleties of this sauce are best with the light outdoorsy flavors of grilled food rather than smoky dishes. MAKES ABOUT 1½ CUPS

1/4 cup vegetable oil or sunflower oil

1 cup minced shallots (from about a dozen medium to large shallots)

1/4 cup dry sherry, such as fino

2 cups apple juice

1/4 cup sherry vinegar

1/2 teaspoon ground cinnamon

1/4 teaspoon ground allspice

1/4 teaspoon ground cloves

1/4 teaspoon kosher salt or coarse sea salt

1. WARM the oil in a large saucepan over medium heat. Stir in the shallots and sauté until translucent and beginning to soften, about 5 minutes. Pour in the sherry and stir to incorporate.

2. ADD the remaining ingredients and cook until the sauce reduces by about half, about 20 minutes. Serve the sauce warm or chilled with poultry. Refrigerate leftovers in a covered container for up to a week.

CHERRY-TEMPRANILLO SAUCE

FOR CONTEMPORARY SMOKED FOOD & GRILLED DISHES

Tempranillo, the grape most famously used in Spain's Rioja wine, is often characterized as having flavors of cherry and plum along with earthy minerality. Those features make it an ideal match with richly flavored duck, at least if there's not an overabundance of smoke. Dried cherries echo the flavors in the wine. You'll want to drink this. MAKES ABOUT 2½ CUPS

> 2 tablespoons olive oil
> 3 tablespoons chopped shallots
> 750-milliliter bottle Rioja or other Tempranillo-based red wine
> 1 cup duck or chicken stock
> 3/4 cup dried cherries
> 2 bay leaves
> Kosher salt or coarse sea salt
> 1 tablespoon unsalted butter

1. WARM the oil in a saucepan over medium heat. Stir in the shallots and cook until softened and translucent, about 5 minutes. Pour in the wine and stock, then add the cherries and bay leaves. Bring the mixture to a boil. Reduce the heat to medium-low and cook until reduced by half, about 30 minutes. Remove the bay leaves. If you would like a smooth sauce, puree it with an immersion blender. Taste and add salt as needed.

2. JUST BEFORE serving warm at the table, whisk in the butter for a final note of flavor. Leftover sauce can be stored in a covered container in the refrigerator for about 5 days.

VARIATION: This sauce can be varied by adding a number of herbs that go well with duck. You might try mint, sage, rosemary, or thyme. Mint should be used fresh, but the others can be used in fresh or dried form. We suggest a couple of tablespoons, minced, of any of the herbs fresh, or 1 tablespoon dried, but follow your taste buds.

QUICK BLACK MOLE

FOR GRILLED DISHES

If you want a great mole, check out Rick Bayless's masterwork, *Authentic Mexican* (William Morrow, 2007). When we want a good mole, but one that takes a slight backseat to grilled chicken or turkey cutlets, we go with this shortcut. Before grilling, flavor the cuts initially with Citrus Paste for Poultry (page 131). MAKES ABOUT 1½ CUPS

> 1 tablespoon sesame oil (not the toasted Asian variety) or almond oil
>
> 1 tablespoon peanut oil
>
> 1 tablespoon minced onion
>
> ¼ cup unsweetened cocoa powder, such as Ghirardelli or Green & Black's
>
> 1 tablespoon ground dried ancho chile
>
> 1 tablespoon ground dried pasilla chile
>
> 1½ cups chicken stock
>
> Minced zest and juice of 1 medium orange

1. WARM the sesame and peanut oils together in a saucepan over medium heat. Stir in the onion and cook until soft and translucent, about 5 minutes.

2. STIR in the cocoa powder and both chiles and cook for 1 more minute. Stir in the stock and orange zest and juice and bring just to a boil. Reduce the heat to medium-low and simmer until the mole is reduced by about one-third, about 20 minutes.

3. SERVE warm or chilled at the table. Refrigerated in a covered container, it will keep for several days.

CELERY CREAM

We don't pair many cream sauces with outdoor food, but it's good to have one in your recipe arsenal. Celery's something of a sleeper, generally relegated to a small supportive role. It can be a standout, though, when surrounded and enhanced by other mild flavors. Lovage, an easy herb to grow, has a celery-like flavor and is another star in this mixture, but isn't commonly found in supermarkets. Look for it at a farmers' market or use an additional tablespoon of celery leaves in its place. **MAKES ABOUT 4 CUPS**

2 cups chopped celery hearts, with leaves

1/2 cup chopped onion

1 tablespoon chopped fresh lovage or additional celery leaves

2 cups chicken stock

1/2 cup whipping cream

Celery salt

White pepper

1. COMBINE the celery, onion, lovage, and stock in a saucepan. Bring to a simmer over medium heat, cover, and cook until the celery is very soft, about 25 minutes. Let the mixture cool briefly and transfer it, in two batches, to a blender and puree each batch.

2. POUR the mixture back into the saucepan through a strainer, pushing on the solids to release as much flavor as possible. Discard the solids. Stir the cream into the sauce base and taste for seasoning, adding celery salt and white pepper as you wish.

3. USE THE sauce warm, spooned onto any simply grilled chicken. The sauce can be cooled and kept refrigerated in a covered container for up to 3 days.

WARM DUCK FAT VINAIGRETTE

If you've been cooking duck, you likely have fat, probably an abundance of it. If you haven't, it's pretty easy to come by in butcher shops or even in jars in gourmet stores. This vinaigrette is a good mate for grilled duck breasts, but it really shines on chicken, especially mildly flavored breasts. You might want to use it as well on grilled vegetables, such as potato slices and sweet potato slices, or corn on the cob. We make this up as we need it.

MAKES ABOUT 3/4 CUP

> 1/4 cup plus 2 tablespoons duck fat
>
> 1 shallot, minced
>
> 1/8 teaspoon crumbled dried thyme
>
> 2 tablespoons vegetable oil or sunflower oil
>
> 1 teaspoon Dijon mustard
>
> 3 tablespoons red wine vinegar or fig vinegar
>
> 1/2 teaspoon kosher salt or coarse sea salt
>
> 1/2 teaspoon freshly cracked black pepper

1. WARM the duck fat in a small skillet over medium-low heat. Stir in the shallot and thyme, cover, and sweat the mixture for 3 minutes. The shallot should become soft but not brown.

2. REMOVE the skillet from the heat and stir in the oil and mustard, which will cool the mixture somewhat. When combined, whisk in the vinegar a bit at a time, and add the salt and pepper. Serve with poultry dishes while warm.

OTHER CONDIMENTS FOR FLAVORING

CHARRED LIME WEDGES

FOR GRILLED DISHES

These versatile garnishes look lovely on the plate with just about anything. We specify that they're best with grilled foods because they are grilled themselves. MAKES 6 SERVINGS

6 medium limes, halved through their equators

1. FIRE up the grill, bringing the temperature to medium (where you can hold your hand an inch or two over the cooking grate for 4 to 5 seconds before you need to pull it away).

2. COAT the lime halves lightly on all sides with vegetable or olive oil spray. Place the limes on the grill grate, cut sides down. Turn the limes with tongs to let them get well marked from the grill on all sides. Serve the limes alongside most any grilled chicken, especially ones with tropical seasonings.

VARIATIONS: Grill lemon wedges in the same fashion and use them with Italian or classic American chicken preparations.

PROSCIUTTO FINISHING SALT

FOR GRILLED DISHES

Yep, it's bacon salt, and you know you want it. This is really a finishing condiment, best sprinkled over grilled chicken as it's coming off the fire. Try it on grilled asparagus or tomatoes, too. MAKES ABOUT 1/2 CUP

6 paper-thin slices prosciutto
1/4 cup kosher salt or coarse sea salt

1. PREHEAT the oven to 375°F. Lay the prosciutto slices flat on a baking sheet. Bake until crispy, about 20 minutes. Drain on paper towels.

2. TRANSFER the prosciutto to a blender with the salt and grind in bursts until fairly fine. Use immediately or store in a covered container in the refrigerator for up to 3 weeks. Sprinkle over food like any other salt.

PEPITA-PEÑO SALSA

FOR GRILLED DISHES

This idea came from the many styles of pipians, or mixtures of seeds and chiles, popular in Mexico. If the pepitas, or pumpkin seeds, that you find are already salted, skip the extra salt at the end. Serve beside grilled chicken parts or duck breasts or spoon over grilled-chicken nachos. MAKES ABOUT 1½ CUPS

1½ cups unsalted pepitas (shelled pumpkin seeds)
1 pickled jalapeño, seeded, and 1 tablespoon pickling liquid from the jar
1 or 2 garlic cloves
½ cup olive oil
Kosher salt or coarse sea salt

1. COMBINE the pepitas, jalapeño, pickling liquid, and garlic in a food processor. Pulse on and off, until you have a coarse puree, about 30 seconds.

2. WITH THE processor running, pour in the oil in a slow, steady stream. Add salt to taste. The salsa is ready to use, spooned on or alongside poultry. To store leftovers, top with a thin film of additional olive oil, cover, and refrigerate for up to 3 weeks.

LYCHEE-PINEAPPLE SALAD

FOR CONTEMPORARY SMOKED FOOD & GRILLED DISHES

Monica Bhide was born in Delhi, India, grew up in the Middle East, and then came to the United States, where she earned two technical graduate degrees before working as an engineer in corporate America for a decade. After all this, Monica decided she really wanted to write, especially about food. Engineering's loss was our gain, as she has a real gift for combining Indian and world flavors in a scrumptious, simple fashion. This vibrant salad, a match with almost any poultry, comes from Monica's book *Modern Spice* **(Simon & Schuster, 2009). Check out her website, monicabhide.com, for many more tasty ideas. MAKES ABOUT 4½ CUPS, ENOUGH TO ACCOMPANY 6 SERVINGS**

1 cup diced fresh lychees, or canned lychees, drained

1 cup diced blood orange or regular orange segments

1 cup diced mango

1/2 cup diced peeled cucumber

1/2 cup diced fresh pineapple

1/2 cup diced peeled pear

Juice of 1 lime (about 2 tablespoons)

1 tablespoon chopped fresh cilantro

1/2 teaspoon crushed hot red chile flakes

Several grinds of black pepper

1/2 teaspoon Indian chaat masala seasoning or kosher salt or coarse sea salt

1. PLACE all of the ingredients except the chaat masala in a large bowl, and toss gently to combine. The salad can sit at room temperature for 30 minutes or be refrigerated, covered, for up to 3 hours.

2. WHEN READY to serve, sprinkle the salad with the chaat masala and serve with chicken or other grilled poultry.

BLACK KALE PESTO

FOR GRILLED DISHES

Kale. It won't go away, so let's do something great with it. This is similar to a classic Genovese pesto, but with the basil switched out for kale. Our favorite to use here is cavolo nero, the Italian kale often referred to as "dino" kale at farmers' markets, but you can use whatever's easily found in your area. This keeps well for days, maybe weeks, maybe forever, as long as oil covers it. Serve it with any grilled poultry. **MAKES ABOUT 2½ CUPS**

2 packed cups chopped kale leaves, tough stem ends discarded

2 garlic cloves

1 cup walnuts

1 cup extra-virgin olive oil

3/4 cup freshly grated Parmigiano-Reggiano cheese

1/2 cup Pecorino Romano cheese

Kosher salt or coarse sea salt, optional

1. PLACE the kale, garlic, and walnuts in a food processor. Process until finely chopped. With the food processor running, pour in the oil in a slow, steady stream. When well combined, add the cheeses and process again. Taste to see if more salt is needed; the cheeses may make the pesto salty enough.

2. USE THE pesto right away, spooned over poultry. To store leftovers, top with a thin film of additional olive oil, cover, and refrigerate.

VARIATION: Use all Parmigiano cheese for a milder, nuttier pesto, or all Pecorino for a stronger cheese tang.

CHUNKY CINNAMON APPLESAUCE

FOR TRADITIONAL BARBECUE, CONTEMPORARY SMOKED FOOD, & GRILLED DISHES

This rustic applesauce just loves a duck—a woodsy, outdoor-cooked duck in particular. Try it on grilled or smoked pork chops, too. MAKES ABOUT 4 CUPS

3 pounds apples, preferably a couple of varieties, peeled, cored, and chopped

1 cup apple cider or juice

3 tablespoons packed brown sugar, or more to taste

2 teaspoons fresh lemon juice

1 teaspoon ground cinnamon, or more to taste

1. PLACE all of the ingredients, using the minimum amounts of brown sugar and cinnamon given, in a large saucepan. Cook the apples over medium heat, giving them a few stirs to combine everything. Bring the mixture to a simmer, then cover, reduce the heat to medium-low, and cook until the apples are very tender but still chunky, about 25 minutes. Cook uncovered for a few more minutes if lots of runny liquid remains.

2. TASTE the applesauce and add more brown sugar and cinnamon if you wish. Serve warm or at room temperature on the side at the table. Leftovers will keep in a covered container in the refrigerator for at least a week.

VARIATION: Make hard applesauce by replacing the unfermented cider with one of the many hard ciders now on the market. Because most hard ciders come in 12-ounce bottles, you can pour in the whole thing and just cook the mixture a few minutes longer than the recipe states. Add 1/2 teaspoon ground allspice to the mix if you wish.

LEBNEH

Almost any kind of cucumber salad or sauce is good with grilled or smoked chicken. Here's a cooling sauce with Middle Eastern roots. Halve the cucumber lengthwise and then scrape away the seeds down the middle—a good task for a melon baller or teaspoon. English cucumbers are not as seedy or weepy as other varieties, but use what is freshest. MAKES ABOUT 2 CUPS

1 cup plain Greek yogurt, preferably a full-fat variety

1/2 cup diced cucumber

1/2 cup dried cherries

1/4 cup chopped walnuts, toasted in a dry skillet until fragrant

1 tablespoon minced fresh dill or 2 teaspoons dried dill

1 teaspoon dried sumac or za'atar, or more to taste

1/4 teaspoon kosher salt or coarse sea salt, or more to taste

Olive oil, about 1 teaspoon

1. COMBINE the yogurt, cucumber, dried cherries, walnuts, and dill in a small bowl. Stir in 1/2 teaspoon of the sumac and the salt.

2. DRIZZLE the oil over the lebneh and sprinkle with the remaining sumac. Serve alongside grilled chicken. Leftover sauce can be stored in a covered container in the refrigerator for up to 3 days.

SINGULAR SEASONINGS FOR
FISH
AND
SHELLFISH

DRY RUBS, PASTES, AND MARINADES

CELERY SPICE

Celery is underappreciated as a vegctable and a seasoning. It makes a subtle but substantial rub for white fish such as tilapia, catfish, snapper, and more. The rub can also be sprinkled onto sea scallops. MAKES ABOUT 3/4 CUP

> 1/4 cup kosher salt or coarse sea salt
> 2 tablespoons celery salt
> 2 tablespoons celery seeds
> 1 tablespoon granulated garlic
> 1 tablespoon smoked sweet paprika
> 1 tablespoon dried lovage or summer savory
> 1 tablespoon crumbled dried thyme

1. STIR together all of the ingredients in a bowl. Sprinkle the rub lightly on fish or shellfish and then massage it in just a bit.

2. ALLOW the seasoned seafood to sit for at least 15 minutes at room temperature, or up to 2 hours wrapped or covered in the refrigerator, prior to cooking. The rub can be stored in a covered container in a cool, dark pantry for up to 3 months.

LEMONY CHILE DILLY RUB

FOR TRADITIONAL BARBECUE, CONTEMPORARY SMOKED FOOD, & GRILLED DISHES

People often think of fish as delicate and believe that it should not be seasoned assertively or cooked with high heat or smoke. We think all of those views are off base. Of course, pristinely fresh seafood brims with flavor of its own, but it can certainly handle well-tailored spicing. Lots of competitors on the barbecue circuit use lemonade powder in their rubs or other seasonings. We find it best in small amounts and with seafood. This rub can be sprinkled onto most anything from the sea destined for outdoor cooking, from whole fish to split lobster tails. **MAKES ABOUT 1 CUP**

> $1/4$ cup kosher salt or coarse sea salt
> $1/4$ cup garlic powder
> $1/4$ cup sweetened lemonade powder
> $1/4$ cup ground dried mild to medium New Mexican red chile
> 1 tablespoon dried dill

1. STIR together all of the ingredients in a bowl. Sprinkle the rub on fish or shellfish and then massage it in lightly.

2. ALLOW the seasoned seafood to sit for at least 15 minutes at room temperature, or up to 2 hours wrapped or covered in the refrigerator, prior to cooking. The rub can be stored in a covered container in a cool, dark pantry for up to 3 months.

spicing TIP A notable exception to our rule about not buying premade seasoning blends is Omnivore Salt, a blend of sea salt and herbs created by Angelo Garro. It's a favorite of culinary stars such as Alice Waters and Michael Pollan. Garro, a blacksmith by trade, learned the recipe from his Sicilian grandmother and made up batches of the salt for friends. They convinced him to run a Kickstarter campaign, which was wildly successful, and the company was born. Order from omnivoresalt.com or heritagefoods usa.com.

BROWN SUGAR AND SPICE RUB

This rub may sound like an odd amalgam, but it's tasty. We like it best on halibut, snapper, and especially salmon. MAKES ABOUT 1 CUP

> 2 tablespoons packed brown sugar
>
> 2 tablespoons yellow mustard seeds
>
> 2 tablespoons coarsely ground coriander seeds
>
> 2 tablespoons dried dill
>
> 2 tablespoons dried dill seeds
>
> 2 tablespoons kosher salt or coarse sea salt
>
> 1 tablespoon ground dried ginger
>
> 1 tablespoon cracked black peppercorns or pink peppercorns
>
> 1 teaspoon ground cinnamon
>
> 1 teaspoon crushed hot red chile flakes

1. STIR together all of the ingredients in a bowl. Sprinkle the rub heavily on fish or shellfish and then massage it in lightly.

2. ALLOW the seasoned seafood to sit for at least 15 minutes at room temperature, or up to 2 hours wrapped or covered in the refrigerator, prior to cooking. The rub can be stored in a covered container in a cool, dark pantry for up to several months.

spicing TIP In the Pacific Northwest, alder is the classic wood for smoking fish, particularly those caught locally. Look for alder chunks or chips at outdoor-cooking stores or online and try using them when you smoke fish. To double your pleasure, make some alder-smoked salt at the same time. Place 1 cup flaky sea salt, such as Maldon, in a shallow smoke-proof dish and put it in the smoker. Check the flavor after 20 or 30 minutes and decide whether it needs more time or not. Use it like any dry rub on wild Pacific fish.

THAI-STYLE WHITE-HOT PEPPERCORN RUB

FOR GRILLED DISHES

White pepper is used for heat and flavor in some dishes from Thailand and other parts of Southeast Asia. Penzeys.com has an especially nice coarse-ground white pepper from Muntok in Indonesia. Use this rub on fish, calamari, shrimp, scallops, and other seafood. MAKES ABOUT 1 CUP

> 1/3 cup coarse-ground white pepper
> 1/3 cup garlic powder
> 1/3 cup kosher salt or coarse sea salt

1. STIR together all of the ingredients in a bowl. Sprinkle the rub lightly on fish or shellfish and then massage it in just a bit.

2. ALLOW the seasoned seafood to sit for at least 15 minutes at room temperature, or up to 2 hours wrapped or covered in the refrigerator, prior to cooking. The rub can be stored in a covered container in a cool, dark pantry for up to several months.

VARIATION: Turn this rub into a seasoning paste by pureeing it with a large bunch of cilantro—leaves, stems, and cleaned roots—and 2 tablespoons of peanut oil or a neutral vegetable oil.

CAMPECHE RECADO

A recado is a seasoning paste used initially by Mayan cooks in Mexico's Yucatán region. As with most other recados, this one is based on achiote, a mixture itself of brick-red annatto seeds and spices. When using a recado for fish, we prefer a greater proportion than usual of fruity juices in the mixture. About 1/2 cup of recado will flavor 2 pounds of snapper, bass, or other mild white fish. **MAKES ABOUT 1¼ CUPS**

> Half of a 3.5-ounce package achiote paste (see Spicing Tip below and on page 15)
> 1/2 medium red onion, chunked
> 1/2 cup packed fresh mint leaves
> 1/4 cup orange juice
> 1/4 cup fresh lime juice
> 2 tablespoons vegetable oil or sunflower oil
> 2 tablespoons ground dried pasilla or ancho chile
> 2 teaspoons kosher salt or coarse sea salt

1. COMBINE all of the ingredients in a food processor until evenly blended. Use immediately or transfer to a covered container and refrigerate for up to 3 weeks.

2. RUB the mixture heavily on fish or shellfish and then massage it in well. Allow the seasoned seafood to sit for at least 30 minutes at room temperature, or up to 2 hours wrapped or covered in the refrigerator, prior to cooking.

spicing **TIP** The achiote paste in this recado tends to stick to a grill's cooking grate. Before grilling, it's always a good idea to have your grate clean, oiled, and hot, but it's essential when cooking with this seasoning and with any fish.

FRESH FENNEL-LEMON PASTE

FOR TRADITIONAL BARBECUE, CONTEMPORARY SMOKED FOOD, & GRILLED DISHES

This is a paste for sure, but one with a difference. The way we prepare it depends on whether we're cooking a whole fish, perhaps a single snapper for the table or a group of trout, or starting with fillets or shellfish. In the case of whole fish, we like to lay out thin slices of fennel and lemon through the fish's middle cavity, so we mix the ingredients by hand to allow the slices to retain their shape. In other cases we simply puree all the ingredients to make a smooth coating to spread on all surfaces. MAKES ABOUT 1 CUP

1 small fennel bulb (about 5 ounces), trimmed and thinly sliced through the stem end

1 medium lemon, thinly sliced

1/3 cup extra-virgin olive oil

2 to 4 garlic cloves, chopped

1 teaspoon kosher salt or coarse sea salt

1. IF YOU plan to use the mixture to flavor a whole fish, combine all of the ingredients gently in a bowl. Tuck the paste-coated fennel and lemon slices into the cleaned cavity of the fish and spread the rest of the paste over the exterior of the fish. Let the fish sit for up to 30 minutes at room temperature before cooking.

2. IF YOU plan to use the mixture to flavor fish fillets or shellfish, combine all of the ingredients in a food processor and puree into a thick paste. Rub the paste on fish fillets or on whole shrimp or scallops. Let the seafood sit for up to 30 minutes at room temperature before cooking.

spicing **TIP** **If you like making mini kebabs, flavor them from the inside as well as the outside by using natural skewers, such as fresh rosemary branches or split pieces of sugar cane, found in many produce sections today. Chunks of firm fish, scallops, and shrimp all take well to natural skewers.**

GREEN CHARMOULA

FOR GRILLED DISHES

This heady seasoning paste traditional to Morocco and other areas of North Africa makes a perfect match with sardines, mackerel, bluefish, and other grilled fish. Set aside about 1/2 cup of it for a table sauce when you serve the fish. Preserved lemons have been salt-packed and can be found in many supermarkets today as well as in specialty food shops. **MAKES ABOUT 1¹/₄ CUPS**

4 garlic cloves, minced

³/₄ teaspoon kosher salt or coarse sea salt

1 cup chopped fresh cilantro

¹/₂ cup chopped fresh flat-leaf parsley

2 tablespoons drained capers

2 tablespoons chopped preserved lemon

2 tablespoons fresh lemon juice

1 teaspoon ground cumin

¹/₂ teaspoon crushed hot red chile flakes

³/₄ cup olive oil

1. MASH the garlic and salt together in a mortar.

2. COMBINE the cilantro and parsley in a food processor and process until the herbs are very finely minced. Add the garlic mixture, capers, preserved lemon, lemon juice, cumin, and chile, and pulse to chop and combine while leaving a bit of texture.

3. STIR the olive oil into the charmoula. Rub the paste on whole fish or fish fillets. Let the fish sit for up to 30 minutes at room temperature before cooking.

WASABI-MISO PASTE

FOR CONTEMPORARY SMOKED FOOD & GRILLED DISHES

We like this paste especially on grilled or smoked tuna steaks or kebabs. The pungent zing of wasabi mixes here with the fermented soy paste known as miso. Miso is typically white, yellow, or red, increasing in strength with the color. The milder but still nicely savory white or yellow miso should be used here, as the red can overwhelm fish. Like many other pastes for seafood, this is best mixed up as you need it. **MAKES ABOUT 1/2 CUP**

> 1/4 cup white or yellow miso paste
> 2 tablespoons soy sauce
> 1 tablespoon water
> 1 tablespoon wasabi (Japanese horseradish) paste or powder, or more to taste
> 1 teaspoon Asian sesame oil
> 1 teaspoon vegetable oil or sunflower oil

1. COMBINE all of the ingredients in a bowl. You may need to use your fingers to mix everything together.

2. SMEAR a thin film of the paste over fish steaks. Let the fish sit for at least 15 minutes at room temperature, or refrigerate wrapped or covered for up to 1 hour, prior to cooking.

GARLICKY BEER MARINADE

Use this hearty souse on shrimp or meaty fish such as mahi-mahi, mackerel, swordfish, bluefish, or catfish. Marinades act pretty quickly on tender fish and shellfish, so don't let them marinate for much more than an hour.

MAKES ABOUT 2 CUPS

12-ounce bottle or can medium-bodied beer

$1/2$ cup water

1 tablespoon liquid from a jar of pickled jalapeños

1 tablespoon vegetable or sunflower oil

6 garlic cloves, minced

$1/2$ teaspoon kosher salt or coarse sea salt

Several splashes of Tabasco sauce, Original Red or green

1. COMBINE all of the ingredients in a bowl or zipper-lock plastic bag.

2. USE within a couple of hours or refrigerate in a covered container and use within a day or two. Cover seafood in the marinade and let sit for at least 15 minutes at room temperature, or refrigerate wrapped or covered up for up to 1 hour, prior to cooking.

> **VARIATION:** Give this marinade a stronger taste of Louisiana by adding a tablespoon of Creole or Cajun seasoning. If your seasoning blend is fairly salty, leave out the salt in the recipe.

WHITE WINE AND WORCESTERSHIRE MARINADE

FOR GRILLED DISHES

This recipe uses Lea & Perrins Marinade for Chicken, which is based on white wine and is lighter than their original Worcestershire sauce. Widely available these days, it works well, we have discovered, with fish preparations, too.

MAKES ABOUT 1½ CUPS

> 1 cup dry white wine
> 1/2 cup Lea & Perrins Marinade for Chicken
> 1 tablespoon fresh lemon juice
> 1 tablespoon vegetable oil or sunflower oil
> 2 or 3 garlic cloves, minced

1. COMBINE all of the ingredients in a bowl or zipper-lock plastic bag. Use within a couple of hours or refrigerate in a covered container and use within a day or two.

2. COVER seafood in the marinade and let sit for at least 15 minutes at room temperature, or refrigerate wrapped or covered for up to 1 hour, prior to cooking.

BEURRE BLANC WHITE WINE MOP

FOR TRADITIONAL BARBECUE & CONTEMPORARY SMOKED FOOD

When we're smoking gently flavored seafood, or when a fish seasoning is already assertive, this is our go-to mop. It's really something of a deconstructed beurre blanc, meaning we never really get around to making the classic French butter sauce, just borrow its ingredients instead.

MAKES ABOUT 2 CUPS

1 cup dry white wine

$1/2$ cup Champagne vinegar

8 tablespoons (1 stick) unsalted butter

2 or 3 shallots, chopped

1 tablespoon compatible dry rub or other seasoning *or* 1 teaspoon kosher salt or coarse sea salt

1. COMBINE all of the ingredients in a saucepan. Heat the mop before you plan to use it initially and keep it warm over low heat between bastes.

2. APPLY to the seafood in the smoker about once every 30 minutes.

VARIATION: Most herbs growing in your garden can add a complementary hint of flavor to this mop. Go as green as you want with parsley, sage, rosemary, thyme, and more.

MALT VINEGAR SPRITZ

FOR CONTEMPORARY SMOKED FOOD

When the seafood is especially rich, like lobster, or has a heavy coating of spice, such as Brown Sugar and Spice Rub (page 172), we opt for this sop.

MAKES ABOUT 2 CUPS

1 cup malt vinegar

3/4 cup seafood or chicken stock

3 tablespoons vegetable oil or sunflower oil

1 tablespoon compatible dry rub or other seasoning *or* 1 teaspoon kosher salt
or coarse sea salt

1. COMBINE all of the ingredients in a saucepan. Heat the mop before you plan to use it initially and keep it warm over low heat between bastes.

2. APPLY to the seafood in the smoker about once every 30 minutes.

CHILE-LEMON BASTE

Try a drizzle of this over fish or shrimp kebabs, or mussels or clams cooked over a hot grill fire until they yawn open. Baste or spoon it on near the end of the grilling. The baste is best made up as you want to use it. Let it sit while you get your seafood cooked for the flavor to bloom. MAKES ABOUT 1/2 CUP

1/2 cup extra-virgin olive oil
Zest from 2 medium lemons
1 garlic clove, sliced
2 teaspoons crushed hot red chile flakes
Pinch of kosher salt or coarse sea salt

1. COMBINE all of the ingredients in a small saucepan. Warm gently over low heat for about 10 minutes. Remove from the heat and let stand at room temperature briefly.

2. SPREAD or spoon on grilled fish or shellfish shortly before it comes off the grill.

SAUCES

BARBECUED SHRIMP BBQ SAUCE

FOR CONTEMPORARY SMOKED FOOD & GRILLED DISHES

Traditionally in New Orleans the famous "barbecued" shrimp are actually sautéed in a skillet. We usually get a little heretical and toss the shrimp on the grill or even smoke them, but in the end we return to home base by serving them with a sauce similar to the skillet version. This sauce is also fantastic on white fish fillets destined for the grill. **MAKES ABOUT 1½ CUPS**

> 8 tablespoons (1 stick) unsalted butter
> ½ cup medium-bodied beer
> Juice of 2 large lemons
> 2 tablespoons cane syrup, such as Steen's, or molasses
> 1 tablespoon Worcestershire sauce
> 1 teaspoon Tabasco or Crystal hot sauce, or more to taste
> 1 teaspoon freshly ground black pepper
> 1 bay leaf
> ½ teaspoon kosher salt or coarse sea salt
> ½ teaspoon dried rosemary or dried thyme

1. MELT the butter in a large saucepan over low heat. Whisk in the rest of the ingredients and cook gently for about 15 minutes.

2. SERVE the sauce warm, for spooning on shrimp or fish, or cool and refrigerate in a covered container. For the best flavor, use it within a week, reheated.

LIME AND BLACK PEPPER MIGNONETTE

FOR CONTEMPORARY SMOKED FOOD & GRILLED DISHES

This finishing sauce perks up the delicious brininess of oysters. Simply put oysters over any form of outdoor fire, and when they pop open, add a small dab of mignonette. MAKES ABOUT 1/2 CUP

> Grated zest and juice of 2 limes
> 2 tablespoons rice vinegar
> 1 garlic clove, minced
> 2 tablespoons coarsely ground black pepper
> 1/8 teaspoon ground allspice
> Splash or two of a favorite hot sauce, optional

1. **STIR** together all of the ingredients in a small bowl.

2. **SPOON** at room temperature into freshly cooked oysters and enjoy right away.

spicing **TIP** It's the acidity in a mignonette that brightens the salinity of the oysters. The topping typically dresses raw oysters but it also zips up cooked ones. The allspice called for here contributes an interesting complexity to the mignonette, but leave it out if it's missing from your spice rack.

PIQUILLO PEPPER ALIOLI

FOR GRILLED DISHES

One of our go-to sauces for years of outdoor cooking has been romesco, a heady Catalonian blend of scarlet but mild piquillo peppers, garlic, bread, almonds, and other seasonings. Here, we've put together a simpler garlic mayonnaise that still offers the elements of romesco that we most crave. Dollops of this are great with any grilled fish fillet or shellfish, and leftovers are quite tasty with grilled vegetables such as eggplant or zucchini slices.

MAKES ABOUT 2 CUPS

> 7- to 8-ounce jar piquillo peppers, drained
> 1 teaspoon minced garlic
> 3/4 cup mayonnaise (not a low-fat variety)
> 2 tablespoons extra-virgin olive oil
> 1/4 teaspoon fresh lemon juice
> 1/4 teaspoon kosher salt or coarse sea salt, or more to taste

1. PUREE the peppers in a food processor. Add the rest of the ingredients to the processor and combine until well blended and smooth.

2. SERVE right way at room temperature, spooned on fish or shellfish. The alioli will keep in a covered container in the refrigerator for up to 3 days, but reheat it gently before using again.

spicing **TIP** Don't let the idea of red peppers in a jar put you off. It's the best way to buy piquillos, which should come from the Navarra region of Spain, where they have been delicately fire-roasted. You can order several good brands online from spanishtable.com or tienda.com, both good sources for other Spanish ingredients as well. In a pinch, you can substitute the same quantity of roasted red bell peppers, although the alioli won't have quite as much character.

PORK FAT HOLLANDAISE IN A BLENDER

This killer sauce, too heavy for traditional barbecue, adds a big punch to grilled or lightly smoked fish or shellfish. It's fantastic on a salmon Benedict made for an outdoor breakfast. MAKES ABOUT 1 CUP

1/2 cup bacon drippings

3 large egg yolks

2 tablespoons fresh lemon juice

1 tablespoon water

Pinch or two of ground cayenne

Kosher salt or coarse sea salt

Freshly ground black pepper

1. MELT the bacon drippings in a small skillet over medium-low heat. Remove from the stove and let the drippings cool a bit.

2. COMBINE the egg yolks, lemon juice, water, cayenne, and a pinch each of salt and black pepper in a blender and puree. With the blender running, pour in the bacon drippings in a very slow, steady stream. Stop when you have a smooth emulsified sauce. Taste and add more salt or pepper if needed. Use immediately alongside or over fish or shellfish.

THAI DIPPING SAUCE

FOR CONTEMPORARY SMOKED FOOD & GRILLED DISHES

Whether you dunk your fish into this sauce or simply dribble it over the sea-food, it contributes tang and sass to grilled meaty fish skewers, calamari, or white fish, or to smoked fare. Try it with shrimp seasoned before cooking in Thai-Style White-Hot Peppercorn Rub (page 173). It's also wonderful on grilled flank steak. MAKES ABOUT 3/4 CUP

1/2 cup Asian fish sauce

3 tablespoons fresh lime juice

1 tablespoon water

2 or 3 crumbled small dried hot chiles, such as bird, cayenne, or de árbol

2 teaspoons granulated sugar

2 garlic cloves, thinly sliced

1. COMBINE all of the ingredients in a small bowl. The sauce can be made earlier in the day you wish to serve it and refrigerated in a covered container. It will, in fact, keep for at least a week, but the lime juice flavor fades quickly, so you'll want to add another squeeze or two of fresh lime before using.

2. SERVE cold or at room temperature with fish or shellfish.

PICKLED JALAPEÑO CREMA

FOR GRILLED DISHES

Creamy and dreamy, this is the ultimate fish or shrimp taco condiment.

MAKES ABOUT 1¹/₄ CUPS

> ¹/₂ cup crème fraîche
>
> ¹/₂ cup plain Greek yogurt, full-fat or 2%
>
> 3 tablespoons mayonnaise
>
> 1 tablespoon fresh lime juice
>
> 2 pickled jalapeños, seeded and chopped, or 1 heaping tablespoon pickled jalapeño slices, chopped
>
> 1 to 2 tablespoons chopped fresh cilantro, optional

1. STIR together all of the ingredients in a small bowl. Serve right away or refrigerate for up to an hour for the flavors to meld.

2. SPOON onto fish or shrimp tacos before serving or pass the sauce at the table.

CAPER AND CORNICHON BUTTER

FOR GRILLED DISHES

This is a buttery blessing for finfish ranging from petrale sole to swordfish, and for shellfish as different as shrimp and mussels. It offers some of the flavor of tartar sauce but with a more delicate finish. MAKES ABOUT ²/₃ CUP

4 tablespoons (¹/₂ stick) unsalted butter, melted

¹/₄ cup extra-virgin olive oil

1 teaspoon fresh lemon juice

¹/₂ teaspoon Dijon mustard

1 tablespoon minced cornichons

2 teaspoons small capers or minced large capers

2 teaspoons minced fresh dill or 1 teaspoon dried dill

¹/₄ teaspoon kosher salt or coarse sea salt

1. COMBINE all of the ingredients in a small bowl and serve right away over fish or shellfish.

2. LEFTOVERS can be refrigerated in a covered container, but reheat the butter before using again.

NORI BUTTER

Nori is dried pressed seaweed formed into paper-like sheets that hold together many forms of sushi. Here it adds a hint of brininess to butter for shrimp, scallops, or crab. Keep extra nori sheets in a zipper-lock plastic bag and store flat in the pantry. MAKES ABOUT 1¼ CUPS

> 5 sheets toasted nori
> ½ cup water
> 12 tablespoons (1½ sticks) unsalted butter
> Kosher salt or coarse sea salt, optional

1. LAY the nori sheets in a shallow baking dish—an 8-inch square dish is perfect. Cover with the water and let sit until soft, about 5 minutes. Transfer the nori and its soaking water to a food processor and pulse to form a smooth paste.

2. MELT the butter in a small saucepan over low heat. Stir in the nori puree. The nori will contribute a mild salty tang to the butter. Add a bit of salt as well if you wish. Use warm over fish or shellfish.

> **VARIATION:** For a slightly more assertive kiss of the sea, opt for anchovies rather than nori in your butter. Use several tablespoons of high-quality anchovy paste, or puree several anchovy fillets, and mix to taste with softened butter.

RED CHILE HONEY BUTTER

This scrumptious compound butter pairs beautifully with salmon and shrimp in particular. MAKES ABOUT 1¼ CUPS

> 8 tablespoons (1 stick) unsalted butter, softened
>
> 3 tablespoons mild-flavored honey
>
> 1 tablespoon ground dried mild red chile, such as New Mexican
>
> ¼ teaspoon kosher salt or coarse sea salt

1. **MIX** all of the ingredients in a medium-size bowl. Use right way, pack into a crock, or roll into a 1- to 2-inch-thick log.

2. **SERVE** warm, at room temperature, or chilled over hot fish or shellfish.

VARIATION: If you wish, substitute agave nectar for the honey.

LEMON AND SHALLOT VINAIGRETTE

We love this fine vinaigrette on grilled baby octopus, smoked bluefish or tuna steak, or any type of grilled or smoked seafood salad. The flavor is best when you mix up the dressing as needed. MAKES ABOUT ³/₄ CUP

1 large shallot, minced

Grated zest of 1 large lemon

3 tablespoons fresh lemon juice

1 teaspoon Dijon mustard

¹/₂ teaspoon kosher salt or coarse sea salt, or more to taste

¹/₂ cup extra-virgin olive oil

1. COMBINE the shallot, lemon zest, and lemon juice in a bowl. Let the mixture stand for about 10 minutes.

2. WHISK in the mustard and ¹/₂ teaspoon salt; when combined, whisk in the oil. Taste to see if more salt is needed. Serve right away, drizzled lightly over fish or shellfish.

VARIATION: Add a couple of teaspoons of chopped fresh lovage, parsley, or chives to the vinaigrette if you wish.

CHINESE XO SAUCE

First popularized in Hong Kong, this rich, meaty sauce for seafood takes its name from high-priced "extra-old" Cognac, indicating its luxury status. You should be able to find the dried shellfish at any Asian market. If the store is out of dried scallops, though, just replace them with additional dried shrimp.

MAKES ABOUT 2 CUPS

> 3 ounces country ham or prosciutto
>
> 1 ounce dried shrimp
>
> 1 ounce dried scallops or additional dried shrimp
>
> 4 garlic cloves
>
> 1 jalapeño or serrano chile, seeded
>
> 1 scallion, limp greens removed, cut in several pieces
>
> Walnut-size nugget of fresh ginger
>
> 1 cup peanut oil, preferably, or vegetable oil
>
> 2 tablespoons soy sauce
>
> 2 teaspoons Asian sesame oil

1. COMBINE the ham, shrimp, scallops, garlic, chile, scallion, and ginger in a food processor and process until finely chopped.

2. WARM the peanut oil in a medium-size skillet over medium-low heat. Scrape the chopped ginger mixture into the skillet and fry until deeply brown, about 15 minutes. Remove the skillet from the heat and let it sit for several minutes to cool.

3. STIR in the soy sauce and the sesame oil. Let the sauce cool fully, then refrigerate it for at least 8 hours to blend the flavors. Use it cool or hot, drizzled lightly over fish or shellfish. The sauce will keep in a covered container in the refrigerator for up to 2 months.

SAUCE CHIEN

FOR GRILLED DISHES

A fiery sauce from the French Caribbean, this is a favorite in the islands on grilled fish, scallops, and shrimp. It's worth it—in looks and taste—to chop the main ingredients to the same small size by hand rather than in a food processor. Wear gloves while mincing the especially pungent Scotch bonnet chile. **MAKES ABOUT 2 CUPS**

> 1 large red onion, very finely chopped by hand
> 3 scallions, very finely chopped by hand
> 1 small carrot, very finely chopped by hand
> Zest of 1 medium lime and juice of 2 medium limes
> 2 tablespoons white vinegar
> 2 tablespoons water
> 2 tablespoons minced fresh thyme
> 1/2 to 1 fresh Scotch bonnet or habanero chile, seeded and very finely minced
> 1/2 teaspoon kosher salt or coarse sea salt
> 1/2 cup vegetable oil or sunflower oil

1. STIR together the onion, scallions, carrot, lime zest and juice, vinegar, water, thyme, chile, and salt in a bowl. Whisk in the oil.

2. THE SAUCE can be used immediately, but we prefer to chill it for 30 to 60 minutes to allow the flavors to meld a bit. It can then be served chilled or warmed a bit to room temperature over fish or shellfish. It will keep in a covered container in the refrigerator for up to a week.

PIRI PIRI VINAIGRETTE

If the Sauce Chien sounds feistier than you like, or has more knife work than you'd prefer, maybe this one's for you. Yes, piri piri is a darned hot chile, too, favored in Brazil and other Portuguese-settled countries, but its fire is tamped down a bit here. Using a bottled piri piri sauce lets you control the amount of heat. It's best mixed up just before you plan to season the seafood at the table. MAKES ABOUT 3/4 CUP

> 1 plump shallot, minced
> 2 tablespoons white vinegar
> 2 teaspoons Asian fish sauce
> 2 teaspoons piri piri sauce, such as Roland's, or more to taste
> 1/2 cup vegetable oil or sunflower oil

1. COMBINE the shallot with the vinegar, fish sauce, and piri piri sauce in a small bowl. Let stand for 10 minutes.

2. WHISK in the oil. Spoon or drizzle right away on grilled fish or shellfish.

SHALLOT YOGURT SAUCE

FOR CONTEMPORARY SMOKED FOOD & GRILLED DISHES

Dab this sauce on smoked salmon, smoked trout, or grilled halibut.

MAKES ABOUT 1 CUP

1 tablespoon extra-virgin olive oil

1/2 cup chopped shallots (from about 3 large shallots)

1 cup plain Greek yogurt, full-fat or 2%

1 tablespoon snipped fresh chives

1. WARM the oil in a small skillet over medium heat. Stir in the shallots, cover, and sweat the shallots until they have softened but have not yet colored, about 2 minutes. Set aside briefly to cool.

2. SPOON the yogurt into a serving dish and stir in the shallot mixture and the chives. Use right away or refrigerate in a covered container for up to 2 days. Serve chilled or at room temperature over fish or shellfish.

OTHER CONDIMENTS FOR FLAVORING

BLACK SESAME SALT

FOR GRILLED DISHES

Treat this like any finishing salt—just sprinkle it over grilled seafood right before bringing the food to the table. MAKES ABOUT 1/2 CUP

1/3 cup black sesame seeds

2 tablespoons kosher salt or coarse sea salt

1 teaspoon coarsely ground black pepper

1. PLACE the sesame seeds in a spice grinder or small food processor. Pulse just a few times, until they are somewhat cracked but not fully ground.

2. DUMP the sesame seeds into a bowl and mix with the salt and pepper. Sprinkle over grilled fish or shellfish just before serving. The salt will keep in a covered container in a cool, dark pantry for up to a month.

TOMATILLO-CUCUMBER SALSA

FOR TRADITIONAL BARBECUE, CONTEMPORARY SMOKED FOOD, & GRILLED DISHES

Surely we aren't the only ones who would be happy if every mango and pine-apple salsa recipe on earth was burned in a giant bonfire to keep them from ever again marring a piece of fish. They are simply too sweet. Here's our idea of what a salsa for fish should taste like. With this salsa, you want some texture, but do chop the ingredients fairly fine so you get a taste of all of them in every tangy bite. MAKES ABOUT 1 1/2 CUPS

6 ounces tomatillos, finely diced

1 red-ripe plum tomato, finely diced

1/2 cup peeled, seeded, and finely diced cucumber

1/4 cup finely diced onion

1 or 2 jalapeño or serrano chiles, seeded and minced

2 tablespoons minced fresh cilantro

1 tablespoon fresh lime juice

2 teaspoons vegetable oil or sunflower oil

1/2 teaspoon kosher salt or coarse sea salt, or more to taste

1. COMBINE all of the ingredients in a bowl. Refrigerate the salsa for at least 15 minutes or preferably 1 hour.

2. SERVE alongside or over fish or shellfish. You can keep any leftovers refrigerated in a covered container, but the flavor fades over a few days.

BASIL–BLACK OLIVE TAPENADE

FOR GRILLED DISHES

Both of us love fresh basil with salmon, other fish, and scallops, but the leaves alone wilt rather quickly. In this recipe, the basil aroma and flavor permeate the tapenade as it melts into whatever fish or shellfish it tops. It's one of the best ways we know to spread the wealth of summer's finest herb.

MAKES ABOUT 1 1/2 CUPS

> 1 cup pitted kalamata olives
> 2/3 cup lightly packed fresh basil leaves
> 2 tablespoons capers
> 1 teaspoon freshly grated orange zest and 2 teaspoons fresh orange juice
> 1/3 cup extra-virgin olive oil

1. COMBINE the olives, basil, capers, and orange zest and juice in a food processor. Pulse to form a thick, coarse puree. With the processor running, pour in the oil in a slow, steady stream.

2. SERVE the tapenade at room temperature alongside or over fish or scallops. To store leftovers, top with a thin slick of additional olive oil, cover, and refrigerate for up to 3 weeks.

GREEN OLIVE AND PRESERVED LEMON RELISH

FOR GRILLED DISHES

This chunky North African–inspired mixture is something like a tapenade minus the pureeing. The preserved lemons, cured in salt, are a common condiment these days at specialty food stores and also at the olive bar in Whole Foods Markets. They are mouth-puckering but practically addictive.

MAKES ABOUT 1½ CUPS

> 1 cup coarsely chopped pitted green olives
> ¼ cup chopped preserved lemon
> 2 garlic cloves, minced
> ¼ cup extra-virgin olive oil

1. STIR together all of the ingredients in a small bowl.

2. SERVE the relish at room temperature alongside or over fish or shellfish. To store leftovers, top with a thin slick of additional olive oil, cover, and refrigerate for up to 3 weeks.

SPICING UP
LAMB, GOAT, VENISON, VEAL, AND RABBIT

DRY RUBS, PASTES, AND MARINADES

TAMARIND RECADO

FOR TRADITIONAL BARBECUE & CONTEMPORARY SMOKED FOOD

A recado is a traditional spice paste of Mexico's Yucatán region. This one gets luscious tang from tamarind paste, available in many supermarkets today, but also a standard ingredient at Mexican, Latin American, and Indian markets. The tamarind also adds a fruity note, enhanced by tomatoes and a bit of honey. This makes enough for a young goat, a leg of lamb, a veal breast, or a venison loin. All benefit from the sweet-sour accent.

MAKES ABOUT 2¹/₂ CUPS

2 medium plum tomatoes

¹/₂ medium onion, thickly sliced

6 garlic cloves, peeled

³/₄ cup tamarind paste

³/₄ cup very hot water

2 tablespoons agave nectar or mild-flavored honey

2 canned chipotle chiles in adobo, plus 1 tablespoon adobo sauce from the can

2 teaspoons vegetable oil or sunflower oil

1 teaspoon kosher salt or coarse sea salt

1. PREHEAT the oven to 425°F. Place a silicone mat or a piece of foil on a baking sheet (for easier cleanup).

2. PLACE the whole tomatoes, the onion slices, and the garlic cloves on the baking sheet. Roast, turning once, until all have softened partially, about 15 minutes. The tomato skin, in particular, should be blackened and blistered and the onion slices should have some color, too. Everything will look pretty sad.

3. PLOP the tomatoes, onion, and garlic in a blender, add the remaining ingredients, and puree. The recado can be used right away or refrigerated in a covered container for up to a week. Rub the paste on lean meat and marinate up to overnight wrapped or covered in the refrigerator prior to cooking.

spicing **TIP** Cocktail bitters liven up all kinds of dishes, not just a Sazerac or Old-Fashioned, and the array of flavors has never been greater. Today you can find bitters featuring black walnut, tamarind, bacon, celery, fennel, lavender, orange, grapefruit, and literally hundreds more, and even bitters aged in former whiskey barrels. Producers make them from an alcohol base with distillations of herbs, roots, and other botanicals. Two of our favorites are Memphis Barbeque Bitters and Jamaican Jerk Bitters, both created by Bill York's Bitter End bitters, based in Santa Fe, New Mexico (bitterendbitters.com). Try them in your barbecue sauces, or add the same company's Mexican Mole Bitters to our Quick Black Mole (page 156). All Bitter End bitters are hand-crafted, from the chopping of the herbs to the labeling of the bottles.

PEPPERY LAMB RUB

FOR TRADITIONAL BARBECUE, CONTEMPORARY SMOKED FOOD, & GRILLED DISHES

Lamb is among the world's most popular meats, but it still remains underappreciated in the United States. The meat is rich without being gamy and it's exceedingly versatile. You can pair lamb with strong spices like cumin, or with rosemary and other potent herbs, and with fruity sauces or other lightly sweet flavorings. In this simple but sassy dry rub, black peppercorns play a lead role. **MAKES ABOUT 1 CUP**

> 1/2 cup freshly ground black pepper
> 2 tablespoons packed brown sugar
> 2 tablespoons ground cinnamon
> 2 tablespoons garlic powder
> 2 tablespoons kosher salt or coarse sea salt
> 2 teaspoons ground cumin

1. STIR together all of the ingredients in a bowl. Sprinkle the rub on cuts of lamb and then massage it well into the meat.

2. ALLOW the seasoned meat to sit for at least 45 minutes at room temperature, or, for large cuts, up to overnight wrapped or covered in the refrigerator, prior to cooking. Store any remaining rub in a covered container in a cool, dark pantry for up to 3 months.

VARIATION: For use with venison, increase the cinnamon by an additional tablespoon.

spicing **TIP** Don't always stick with the familiar chops and leg when selecting lamb. The shoulder or racks of ribs are good for the smoker, as is a cut called lamb top, from high up on the leg. All can be seasoned with dry rubs, pastes, or marinades. If you're a lover of garlic, poke slices of garlic into every cranny, along with any other flavoring of your choice.

ZESTY RUB FOR VEAL, VENISON, AND RABBIT

FOR CONTEMPORARY SMOKED FOOD & GRILLED DISHES

Veal and rabbit are milder meats than venison, but all three combine well with warm spices such as ginger, dried orange peel, paprika, and a bit of chile. We like this on small cuts of all three, whether slowly cooked by smoke or quickly grilled. MAKES ABOUT 3/4 CUP

> 1/4 cup kosher salt or coarse sea salt
>
> 3 tablespoons ground dried ginger
>
> 2 tablespoons ground coriander
>
> 2 tablespoons dried orange zest
>
> 1 tablespoon turbinado sugar
>
> 1 tablespoon smoked paprika
>
> 1 tablespoon ground dried mild red chile, such as ancho or New Mexican
>
> 1 teaspoon crushed hot red chile flakes

1. STIR together all of the ingredients in a bowl. Sprinkle the rub on cuts of veal, venison, or rabbit and then massage it well into the meat.

2. ALLOW the seasoned meat to sit for at least 45 minutes at room temperature, or, for large cuts, up to overnight wrapped or covered in the refrigerator, prior to cooking. Store any remaining rub in a covered container in a cool, dark pantry for up to 3 months.

spicing **TIP** The lean meats featured in this chapter often benefit from herbal and fruity flavorings, and a hint or more of pungency. With the few exceptions we feature, dry rubs are less optimal for advance seasoning than pastes and marinades that add moistness as well as flavor.

BAHARAT RUB

It's no surprise that Middle Eastern cultures that prize lamb have specialized in seasonings that marry well with the meat. Baharat generally combines black pepper and cumin with other spices as diverse as sumac, rose petals, and saffron. You can pick up the mixture in some spice stores and in Middle Eastern markets, but here's a good starting point for your own homemade version. MAKES ABOUT 1 CUP

3 tablespoons black peppercorns

2 tablespoons cumin seeds

2 tablespoons coriander seeds

1 tablespoon fennel seeds

2 tablespoons sweet paprika

2 tablespoons dried mint

2 tablespoons ground cinnamon

1 tablespoon kosher salt or coarse sea salt

1 teaspoon freshly grated nutmeg

1. GRIND the peppercorns with the cumin, coriander, and fennel seeds in a spice mill or mortar, in batches if necessary. Pour the mixture into a bowl and mix in the remaining ingredients.

2. MASSAGE the rub onto lamb and let sit for at least 30 minutes at room temperature, or, for large cuts, up to overnight wrapped or covered in the refrigerator, prior to cooking. Leftover rub will keep in a covered container in a cool, dark pantry for up to 3 months.

VARIATION: To turn this into a seasoning paste that clings nicely to shish kebabs, mix the dry seasonings in a food processor with 1/2 medium onion and enough olive oil to make a thin paste.

spicing TIP Za'atar, a centuries-old spice blend from the Middle East, makes a good dry rub for lamb. The mixture usually includes dried thyme, nutty sesame seeds, and sumac, a tangy spice that adds an acidic note.

TIM BYRES'S CABRITO AND LAMB SPICE

FOR TRADITIONAL BARBECUE, CONTEMPORARY SMOKED FOOD, & GRILLED DISHES

Chef Tim has a Dallas restaurant called Smoke and a James Beard Foundation award-winning book by the same name (Rizzoli, 2013). He also has a heckuva good dry rub mixture for lamb and young goat. It incorporates flavors from Central America, the Caribbean, and West Africa. You have to toast a few spices and measure out quite a few others, but Tim's done the hard work of figuring it out in the first place. He says to make sure you dump the toasted spices out of the skillet as soon as they are fragrant so that they don't sit in the hot pan and burn. That's good advice any time you're toasting spices. **MAKES ABOUT 3 CUPS**

1/2 cup cumin seeds

2 tablespoons coriander seeds

2 tablespoons yellow mustard seeds

2 tablespoons black peppercorns

1 tablespoon caraway seeds

1 cup packed brown sugar

1/2 cup kosher salt or coarse sea salt

2 tablespoons granulated garlic

2 tablespoons granulated onion

2 tablespoons curry powder

1 tablespoon granulated sugar

1 tablespoon crumbled dried sage

1 tablespoon crumbled dried thyme

1 1/2 teaspoons ground cayenne pepper

1. IN A medium-size dry skillet, toast the cumin, coriander, and mustard seeds with the peppercorns over high heat until they are fragrant and start to pop, about 5 minutes. Transfer the toasted seeds to a small bowl and set aside to cool.

2. IN A large bowl, combine the remaining ingredients. When the toasted spices have cooled, grind them to a medium-fine coarseness in a spice grinder, in batches if necessary. You can do this in a mortar with a pestle, too, but it's a lot of grinding by hand. Mix the ground toasted spices into the large bowl of remaining ingredients. Rub the mixture between your palms to break up any clumps.

3. MASSAGE the rub onto cabrito or lamb and let sit for at least 30 minutes at room temperature, or, for large cuts, up to overnight wrapped or covered in the refrigerator, prior to cooking. Store any remaining rub in a covered container in a cool, dark pantry for up to 3 months.

SAGE-LEMON PASTE

FOR TRADITIONAL BARBECUE & CONTEMPORARY SMOKED FOOD

It was the use of this seasoning paste some years ago on young goat that convinced us of this book's theme: that it really pays to match the flavoring to the kind of meat and outdoor cooking technique. We were barbecuing two goats, one with a traditional barbecue spice rub, the other with this herb paste we whipped up because our nearby garden was overflowing with sage. The paste worked far better on the lean meat than the dry rub. If you're not cooking a whole goat, or meat of similar weight, you can cut the recipe in half. **MAKES ABOUT 4 CUPS**

> 3 cups packed fresh sage leaves
> Grated zest of 2 lemons
> 1 garlic head, cloves peeled
> 1 tablespoon kosher salt or coarse sea salt
> 1 tablespoon ground cumin, optional
> 2 cups olive oil

1. COMBINE the sage, lemon zest, garlic, salt, and cumin, if you are using it, in a food processor. Pulse until the sage and garlic are chopped very fine.

2. WITH THE processor running, pour in the oil in a slow, steady stream until a thick paste forms. Rub the paste on young goat or lamb and refrigerate wrapped or covered for at least 12 hours and up to 24 hours prior to cooking.

VARIATION: For other herbal options, leave out the cumin and use fresh mint instead of sage, or replace half of the sage with fresh rosemary.

spicing TIP Young goat, called by the Spanish name cabrito in much of the Southwest, and sometimes by the French-derived moniker chevon in other areas, is lean, tender, and a bit like a robust lamb in flavor. We prefer cooking it slow and low, rather than over a high-heat fire. A moist seasoning like this Sage-Lemon Paste or the Tamarind Recado (page 206) will help shield the meat from drying out.

RED WINE MARINADE FOR LAMB AND GAME MEATS

We drink red wine with lamb and venison, so it makes sense to us to share it with the meat. Strong aromatics—green peppercorns, anchovy paste, and piney juniper berries—pair pleasantly with the mild assertiveness character-istic of lamb and farm-raised venison. MAKES ABOUT 2 CUPS

13/4 cups dry red wine

2 tablespoons packed brown sugar

2 tablespoons olive oil

1 tablespoon drained green peppercorns

2 teaspoons juniper berries, bruised with the side of a chef's knife

1 teaspoon anchovy paste or kosher salt or coarse sea salt

1 teaspoon freshly ground black pepper

1. WHISK together all of the ingredients in a bowl or combine them in a large zipper-lock plastic bag. Use the marinade right away or refrigerate it in a covered container for up to 2 days.

2. POUR the marinade over the lamb or other meat and let it sit for at least 30 minutes at room temperature, or refrigerate wrapped or covered up to overnight, prior to cooking.

VARIATION: If you're keen on garlic flavor, eliminate 1 of the 2 tablespoons of brown sugar and all of the juniper berries. Add 4 or more chopped garlic cloves to the marinade.

FRUITY MUSTARD MARINADE

This marinade tastes terrific on anything from veal breast to chops, and venison backstrap to pot roast. Nearly any fruit can be a candidate to flavor these meats before or after cooking. The hit of mustard protects the marinade from any cloying sweetness. MAKES ABOUT 2 CUPS

> $1^1/_2$ cups cran-apple or sweetened cranberry juice
> $^1/_4$ cup dry or semi-dry sherry
> $^1/_4$ cup Dijon mustard
> 2 tablespoons minced fresh ginger
> 1 tablespoon vegetable oil
> 1 teaspoon kosher salt or coarse sea salt
> 1 teaspoon ground cayenne, optional

1. WHISK together all of the ingredients in a bowl or combine them in a large zipper-lock plastic bag.

2. POUR the marinade over the meat and let sit for at least 30 minutes at room temperature, or refrigerate wrapped or covered up to overnight, prior to cooking.

> **VARIATION:** For an even fruitier marinade, suitable for the low heat of smoke cooking, add several tablespoons of currant liqueur to the marinade. This would be especially good on meat served with Roasted Grapes (page 235) or Blackberry-Sage Sauce (page 226).

MOPS AND BASTES

ANCHO-CINNAMON SPLASH

FOR TRADITIONAL BARBECUE & CONTEMPORARY SMOKED FOOD

This moderately spicy mop works well with meat flavored before cooking with such different blends as Tamarind Recado (page 206) or Zesty Rub for Veal, Venison, and Rabbit (page 209). MAKES ABOUT 3¹/₂ CUPS

> 12-ounce bottle or can decent-quality beer
> 1 cup cider vinegar or white vinegar
> 1 cup water
> ¹/₄ cup vegetable or sunflower oil
> ¹/₄ cup ground dried ancho chile
> 2 tablespoons ground cinnamon
> 1 tablespoon packed brown sugar
> 1 garlic head, cloves peeled and halved horizontally
> 2 tablespoons kosher salt or coarse sea salt

1. COMBINE all of the ingredients in a saucepan.

2. HEAT the mop before you plan to use it initially and keep it warm over low heat between bastes. Apply to the meat once or twice an hour.

> spicing **TIP** **Because all of the meats in this chapter are on the lean side, when barbecuing them use a mop with a good proportion of oil to help keep them moist—at least 1 tablespoon per cup of liquid in the mop.**

CIDER VINEGAR AND POMEGRANATE MOLASSES MOP

FOR CONTEMPORARY SMOKED FOOD

We remember first learning about and buying Middle Eastern pomegranate molasses a couple of decades ago from a faraway source, probably in New York. When we read about it, we immediately loved the idea of a thick sweet-sour pomegranate condiment. We had to buy six bottles of it in those pre-Internet days, and the bottles lasted us for years. Now it's available in many supermarkets, including Whole Foods, in Middle Eastern markets, and certainly online. This tangy mop goes well with lamb, venison, young goat, or rabbit. **MAKES ABOUT 3½ CUPS**

> 2 cups cider vinegar
> 1 cup water
> ¼ cup pomegranate molasses
> ¼ cup olive oil
> 2 tablespoons kosher salt or coarse sea salt
> 1 tablespoon za'atar (see Spicing Tip, page 210) or compatible dry rub seasoning

1. COMBINE all of the ingredients in a saucepan.

2. HEAT the mop before you plan to use it initially and keep it warm over low heat between bastes. Apply to the meat once or twice an hour.

COCONUT WATER MOP

FOR TRADITIONAL BARBECUE & CONTEMPORARY SMOKED FOOD

Just as it sounds, coconut water is the refreshing liquid from inside a coconut. Your mop will smell like a day at the beach. Along with that heavenly scent, meat that you drizzle it over will take on quite a deep bronze hue, as if it went to the tropics for vacation. Whacking open your own coconut is fun and will impress the heck out of your friends, but it's also okay to buy the water ready to use from a store. **MAKES ABOUT 3 CUPS**

2 cups coconut water, such as Harmless Harvest
1 cup water
2 tablespoons coconut oil
Juice of 1 medium lime, optional

1. COMBINE all of the ingredients in a saucepan.

2. HEAT the mop before you plan to use it initially and keep it warm over low heat between bastes. Apply to the meat once or twice an hour.

RED WINE SOP

FOR CONTEMPORARY SMOKED FOOD

This recipe calls for dried rosemary or sage, but if you flavored the meat in advance with a different herb in a rub, paste, or marinade, use the same herb again in this mopping liquid. It's a principle that is broadly applicable in creating and tailoring mops and bastes. **MAKES ABOUT 3 CUPS**

2 cups dry red wine

1/2 cup beef or lamb stock

1/4 cup olive oil

2 tablespoons kosher salt or coarse sea salt

2 bay leaves

2 garlic cloves, sliced

1 tablespoon dried rosemary or sage, or other compatible dried herb

1 teaspoon anchovy paste or kosher salt or coarse sea salt

1. COMBINE all of the ingredients in a saucepan.

2. HEAT the mop before you plan to use it initially and keep it warm over low heat between bastes. Apply to the meat once or twice an hour.

CURRY IN A HURRY BASTE

FOR GRILLED DISHES

We developed this as a baste to add a pleasantly mild curry flavor to lamb chops, lamb kebabs, or other small cuts of lamb on the grill. Cilantro-Mint Chutney (page 237) makes a tasty table condiment for lamb prepared with this baste. **MAKES ABOUT 2 CUPS**

1¹/₂ cups carrot juice
¹/₄ cup cider vinegar
2 tablespoons ghee (clarified butter; see Spicing Tip, page 258) or unsalted butter
1 tablespoon curry powder
Kosher salt or coarse sea salt, optional

1. COMBINE all of the ingredients in a saucepan and warm over medium heat.

2. BASTE the lamb with the blend twice during the grilling, once early and again near the end.

spicing TIP Curry powder is a simple, mostly American adaptation of Indian masala, and it is indeed a good solution when you want curry flavor quickly. We find most grocery store brands pretty bland, however. Try to buy curry powder from a spice shop where you can sample the mixtures. We like all of the Penzeys curry powders we have tried (penzeys.com); for lamb, and this baste in particular, we recommend the highly aromatic Hot Curry Powder or Rogan Josh Seasoning.

SAUCES

MEZCALITO ORANGE SAUCE

FOR CONTEMPORARY SMOKED FOOD & GRILLED DISHES

A little smoky mezcal plus a little sweet orange equal a lot of great taste. You don't need to use a premium mezcal for this, but don't bother with the varieties that feature a worm at the bottom of the bottle. The sauce tastes splendid on lamb, cabrito, or venison. **MAKES ABOUT 1 CUP**

> 1 cup mezcal
> 1/2 cup orange juice
> 1/4 cup orange liqueur, such as Triple Sec
> 1/4 teaspoon kosher salt or coarse sea salt
> 2 tablespoons unsalted butter or lard

1. COMBINE the mezcal, orange juice, orange liqueur, and salt in a saucepan and warm over medium heat. Simmer the mixture for about 10 minutes.

2. WHISK the butter into the sauce and serve warm to spoon over meat. Leftovers will keep for a week in a covered jar in the refrigerator, but should be reheated before serving again.

SASSY HOISIN BARBECUE SAUCE

FOR TRADITIONAL BARBECUE, CONTEMPORARY SMOKED FOOD, & GRILLED DISHES

These sweet and savory, somewhat Chinese flavors give a lift to any cut of lamb, from a barbecued shoulder to a grilled rack of lamb ribs or leg of lamb.

MAKES ABOUT 1 CUP

1/2 cup hoisin sauce

1/4 cup plum preserves

2 tablespoons soy sauce

2 tablespoons water

1 tablespoon ketchup or tomato-based barbecue sauce

1 teaspoon toasted sesame oil

1/2 to 1 teaspoon Asian chile oil or sriracha

1. COMBINE the hoisin sauce, preserves, soy sauce, water, and ketchup in a saucepan and warm over medium heat. Simmer the mixture for about 10 minutes.

2. WHISK the sesame oil and chile oil into the sauce and serve warm with lamb. Leftovers will keep for a week in a covered jar in the refrigerator, but should be reheated before serving again.

MAGIC BLACK HOT SAUCE

FOR TRADITIONAL BARBECUE

Back in the nineteenth century, many settlers in the vicinity of Owensboro, Kentucky, raised sheep for wool. When the sheep got old and were too tough for routine cooking, the herders barbecued the meat. Owensboro restaurants such as Moonlite Bar-B-Q Inn and Old Hickory Bar-B-Que still barbecue mutton the way it was done in the past. A dark vinegary mixture, often with Worcestershire and some cayenne for heat, was commonly used as a barbecue baste and as a table sauce as well. Because the sauce was thin, locals called it a "dip." It still works wonders today for barbecued lamb, yearling lamb, or mutton. MAKES ABOUT 2 CUPS

> 1 cup white vinegar
> 1 cup Worcestershire sauce
> 1/4 cup water
> 2 tablespoons Tabasco sauce, preferably Original Red
> 1 tablespoon ground cayenne
> 1 tablespoon packed dark brown sugar
> 1 teaspoon kosher salt or coarse sea salt
> 1 teaspoon ground white pepper

1. COMBINE all of the ingredients in a saucepan and warm over medium heat. Simmer the mixture for about 10 minutes.

2. SERVE hot or at room temperature. It will keep for weeks in a covered jar or bottle in the refrigerator.

BLACKBERRY-SAGE SAUCE

FOR GRILLED DISHES

Use blackberries, loganberries, or marionberries for this sauce, scrumptious with rabbit or venison in particular. We like the robust flavor from the larger amount of sage suggested, but feel free to use the smaller quantity for a gentler herbal note. MAKES ABOUT 1½ CUPS

> 2 tablespoons unsalted butter
> 1 large shallot, minced
> 2 cups chicken stock
> 2 cups fresh or frozen blackberries, loganberries, or marionberries
> 1 to 2 teaspoons crumbled dried sage
> Kosher salt or coarse sea salt
> Blackberry jelly or jam, or brown sugar, optional

1. **MELT** the butter in a saucepan over medium heat. Stir in the shallot and sauté until soft, about 3 minutes. Add the stock, berries, and sage and bring to a boil. Reduce the heat to low and simmer until the berries have disintegrated, about 20 more minutes.

2. **STRAIN** the sauce into a bowl, pressing on the solids to extract from them as much liquid as possible. Return the sauce to the saucepan and season to taste with salt. If the sauce tastes overly tart, stir in a bit of jelly or brown sugar, if you wish, to balance the flavor.

3. **CONTINUE** cooking the sauce over low heat until it has thickened and reduced to about 1½ cups. The sauce can be used right away, or cooled and refrigerated in a covered container for a day. Reheat the sauce before serving spooned over rabbit or venison.

CHARRED SERRANO HOT SAUCE

Lamb and young goat have been traditional meats of the American Southwest since long before beef became the region's iconic choice. This salsa can accompany both lamb and kid. If you can't find serrano chiles, you can use jalapeños in a pinch; the heat is similar. Whip this up a day ahead of when you want to use it. **MAKES ABOUT 1¹/₂ CUPS**

8 fresh serrano chiles

1 fresh mild green chile, such as New Mexican or poblano

1 cup white vinegar

¹/₂ cup water

2 tablespoons shelled pumpkin seeds (pepitas)

2 tablespoons minced onion

4 garlic cloves

1¹/₂ teaspoons kosher salt or coarse sea salt

1. CHAR 4 of the serranos and the mild chile over a stove burner or hot grill, turning to blacken on all sides. When the chiles are cool enough to handle, remove the stems and seeds, but not the blackened peel. Remove the stems and seeds from the 4 uncharred serranos, too.

2. PLOP all of the chiles in a blender with the rest of the ingredients. Puree until the sauce is smooth, about 2 minutes. Refrigerate the sauce for at least 8 hours. Reblend the sauce and then strain it through a fine-mesh strainer into a bottle.

3. SERVE the sauce cold on the side with dinner, or store in a covered container in the refrigerator for later use—it keeps for weeks.

POMEGRANATE MOLASSES AND BLACK PEPPER VINAIGRETTE

Pomegranate molasses, a cooked-down syrup of pomegranate juice with some sugar, is a fabulous sweet-tart condiment, as tasty here as in the mop featured earlier in this chapter (page 218). Given its Middle Eastern origins, it's a perfect mate for lamb in particular, but it also tastes great on venison or even duck breasts. MAKES ABOUT 1¼ CUPS

1/4 cup pomegranate molasses

2 tablespoons red wine vinegar

2 teaspoons Dijon mustard

1 teaspoon freshly cracked black pepper

1/2 teaspoon brown sugar

1/2 teaspoon kosher salt or coarse sea salt, or more to taste

1/2 cup extra-virgin olive oil

1/4 cup vegetable oil or sunflower oil

1. WHISK together the molasses, vinegar, mustard, pepper, brown sugar, and salt in a deep bowl.

2. WHEN WELL blended, whisk in both oils. The vinaigrette should emulsify, or thicken and bind together. Use at room temperature as a table sauce, or refrigerate in a covered container for up to 3 days and use chilled.

spicing **TIP** **Cracked pepper is a very coarsely ground pepper. You can see that little chunks of it came off something that was once round. If your pepper mill does not have a very coarse setting on it, you can crack peppercorns by putting them in a small plastic bag and then giving them a few whacks with the smooth side of a meat mallet.**

HERBED YOGURT SAUCE

FOR CONTEMPORARY SMOKED FOOD & GRILLED DISHES

Throughout the eastern Mediterranean and Middle East, various yogurt sauces—cacik, tzatziki, lebneh—combine all manner of herbs and spices, and sometimes fruits, vegetables, and nuts, too. We have a Lebneh (page 167) in the poultry chapter that includes all of these ingredients. This yogurt sauce is less complex and just right on more highly flavored lamb. The sauce makes enough to accompany a leg of lamb or a big batch of lamb burgers.

MAKES ABOUT 1¼ CUPS

> 1 cup plain full-fat Greek yogurt
> 2 tablespoons chopped fresh dill
> 2 tablespoons chopped fresh mint
> 2 teaspoons olive oil
> 1 teaspoon za'atar (see Spicing Tip, page 210) or dried sumac, optional

1. STIR together all of the ingredients in a medium-size bowl. Refrigerate for about 30 minutes to bolster the flavor.

2. SERVE the sauce chilled or at room temperature dolloped over sliced lamb or lamb burgers.

spicing TIP Tanzeya is a Middle Eastern stewed mixture of dried fruit and exotic spices that is similar to chutney. A small Brooklyn business called NYSHUK creates a scrumptious version of the sweet-savory condiment, made with apricots, figs, raisins, prunes, and more. *Shuk* means "market" in Hebrew, and husband-wife team Ron and Leetal Arazi see markets as essential to community. They sell tanzeya on their website, nyshuk.com, along with a couple of other condiments. Tanzeya is a pure delight with grilled or smoked lamb, but it can also be mixed into plain yogurt to make another type of yogurt-based sauce.

HARISSA-HONEY GLAZE

Slather this garlicky chile-and-honey sauce onto grilled lamb chops, kebabs, or leg of lamb in the last few minutes of cooking and serve it at the table, too. It goes especially well with meat seasoned in advance with Peppery Lamb Rub (page 208) or Baharat Rub (page 210). You can start with a cup of store-bought harissa, but it's pretty cool to tell your guests you made it from scratch. You can put the harissa together a few days ahead if you wish, then simply combine it with the honey and lemon before you grill. MAKES ABOUT 1¹/₂ CUPS

HARISSA PASTE

4 ounces dried red chiles, preferably a combination of some hot and some mild, such as 3 ounces New Mexican or ancho pods and 1 ounce chiles de árbol

1 teaspoon caraway seeds

¹/₂ teaspoon coriander seeds

¹/₂ teaspoon cumin seeds

4 to 6 garlic cloves

1 teaspoon crumbled dried mint

1 teaspoon kosher salt or coarse sea salt

GLAZE

3 tablespoons mild-flavored honey

Juice of 1 medium lemon

1. MAKE the harissa: Warm a skillet over medium heat. Place the chiles in the skillet and toast quickly on each side, just until fragrant. Transfer the chiles to a bowl and pour in enough hot water to cover them.

2. POUR the caraway seeds, coriander seeds, and cumin seeds into the skillet and toast them quickly, just until they are fragrant. Grind the seeds in a spice grinder or mortar until fine.

3. WHEN THE chiles have softened, after about 10 minutes, drain them and transfer them to a food processor. Add the ground seeds to the processor along with the garlic,

mint, and salt. Puree the mixture until smooth, about 1 minute. The harissa can be refrigerated in a covered container for several weeks.

4. MAKE the glaze: Combine the harissa with the honey and lemon juice. If the mixture is too thick to easily brush on lamb, add water as needed to achieve the proper texture. Baste the meat with the glaze in the last few minutes of cooking and serve the remainder on the side as a table sauce. The glaze can be kept in a covered container in the refrigerator for up to 3 weeks.

LADOLEMONO

FOR CONTEMPORARY SMOKED FOOD & GRILLED DISHES

This Greek-inspired mixture is essentially a vinaigrette punched up with lemon, oregano, and garlic. Lamb loves it. It also cuddles well with grilled seafood. MAKES ABOUT 1¹/₄ CUPS

1/3 cup fresh lemon juice

2 teaspoons Dijon mustard

2 teaspoons crumbled dried oregano

1 garlic clove, minced

1/2 teaspoon kosher salt or coarse sea salt, or more to taste

2/3 cup extra-virgin olive oil

Freshly ground black pepper

1. WHISK together the lemon juice, mustard, oregano, garlic, and salt in a deep bowl. When blended, whisk in the oil and add pepper to taste.

2. USE the ladolemono right away or let sit at room temperature for up to an hour. Whisk it again to combine well. Drizzle a small amount over lamb before serving.

spicing **TIP** Ladolemono is pretty simple to make. If you're looking for an even simpler way to sauce lamb, just combine some hoisin sauce with enough soy sauce to make it spoonable. You're good to go.

SAUCE PALOISE

FOR CONTEMPORARY SMOKED FOOD & GRILLED DISHES

Paloise takes its name from the French city of Pau, and it's another traditional sauce that can make you look like a pro in your own backyard. An elegant Hollandaise-style sauce flavored beautifully with mint, it's oh-so-fabulous with lamb loin or rib chops, or slices of leg of lamb. You need to make the sauce shortly before serving, though you can do the initial reduction of wine and vinegar ahead if you like. (If you really need to hold the sauce, keep it warm in a thermos.) The sauce requires the cook's full attention for up to 8 minutes, a small sacrifice for such luxury. MAKES ABOUT 1 CUP

1/4 cup dry white wine
2 tablespoons white wine vinegar
2 tablespoons minced shallots
2 tablespoons chopped fresh mint stems
3 large egg yolks
8 tablespoons (1 stick) unsalted butter, cut in 16 equal chunks
Pinch of white pepper
Kosher salt or coarse salt
1 tablespoon whole fresh mint leaves

1. COMBINE the wine, vinegar, shallots, and chopped mint stems in a medium-size saucepan over medium heat. Reduce the mixture until 2 tablespoons of liquid remain. Strain the liquid, discarding the solids, and return the liquid to the saucepan.

2. WHISK in the egg yolks. Warm gently over low heat, whisking continuously. When you can begin to see trails across the pan's bottom as you make the whisking strokes, add the butter, a chunk at a time. Whisk each chunk in fully before adding the next one, but introduce them more or less continuously. To avoid overheating, take the pan off the heat while incorporating about every other chunk. Season to taste with white pepper and salt just before you are ready to remove the sauce from the heat for the last time. The sauce is ready when it is thick, silky, and still spoonable, 5 to 8 minutes total.

3. MINCE the mint leaves at the last minute and stir them into the sauce. Serve warm, blanketing lamb.

AGRODOLCE SAUCE

A time-honored sweet-sour sauce of Italy, especially Sicily, agrodolce richly complements venison or rabbit. It combines sugar and vinegar for the sweet and sour elements, and a few other flavorings to build on the basics.

MAKES ABOUT 1½ CUPS

> 1/4 cup extra-virgin olive oil
>
> 2 large shallots, chopped
>
> 1 garlic clove, minced
>
> 2 tablespoons dry red wine
>
> 1 cup inexpensive balsamic vinegar
>
> 1/3 cup water
>
> 2 tablespoons granulated sugar
>
> 1 bay leaf
>
> 2 tablespoons dried currants
>
> 2 tablespoons capers
>
> 1 teaspoon kosher salt or coarse sea salt, or more to taste
>
> 1/4 teaspoon freshly ground black pepper

1. WARM the oil in a saucepan over medium heat. Add the shallots and garlic and sauté until they are translucent and beginning to soften, about 5 minutes. Pour in the wine carefully, and let it sputter and mostly evaporate.

2. STIR in the vinegar, water, sugar, and bay leaf. Bring the mixture just to a boil, then reduce the heat to a simmer and cook for 15 minutes. Add the currants, capers, salt, and pepper and cook until reduced by about one-third, about 10 minutes more. Remove and discard the bay leaf. Taste to see if more salt is needed.

3. SERVE the sauce warm with venison or rabbit. The sauce can be cooled and refrigerated in a covered container for up to 2 days, but reheat gently before serving.

> **VARIATIONS:** Add about 1/4 cup toasted pine nuts, or switch out the currants for golden raisins.

OTHER CONDIMENTS FOR FLAVORING

ROASTED GRAPES

Fruity ingredients always make a good pairing with lamb and venison, especially when they have a note of savoriness, which olive oil provides here. If you have a grill fired up, you can do the roasting in a covered grill rather than the oven. This is enough grapes to accompany six servings of elk tenderloin or lamb chops. **MAKES ABOUT 2 CUPS**

1/4 cup dry or sweet red wine
1 tablespoon olive oil
2 teaspoons granulated sugar
1 pound seedless red grapes

1. PREHEAT the oven to 400°F. Select a shallow baking dish in which the grapes will fit in a single layer.

2. WHISK together the wine, oil, and sugar in a large bowl, then add the grapes and toss to coat. Spoon the grapes into the baking dish. Roast the grapes, stirring once, until the grapes have begun to soften and the skins shrivel a bit, about 25 minutes. The grapes should still hold their shapes, though somewhat loosely.

3. THE PAN liquid will have formed a syrup. Serve spoonfuls of the grapes with some of the syrup alongside the meat. The grape mixture can be refrigerated in a covered container for up to 5 days, but reheat gently before serving.

VARIATIONS: Add 1 teaspoon minced fresh thyme, 1/2 teaspoon ground cinnamon, or other compatible seasoning from your main ingredient to the grape mixture before roasting.

EASY BALSAMIC JELLY

FOR GRILLED DISHES

We had planned to provide a recipe here for a standard type of jelly that you would can, using pectin as the thickener. When researching various methods for making jellies, we came across a load of online recipes using gelatin as the thickener. It makes quite a fun and jiggly jelly, and one that's easy to prepare in small batches. The jelly can be cut into jewel-like cubes to accompany lamb burgers, other lamb dishes, and venison or rabbit preparations.

MAKES ABOUT 1 1/2 CUPS

1 1/4 cups inexpensive balsamic vinegar or strawberry or raspberry balsamic vinegar

2 teaspoons unflavored gelatin

1/4 cup granulated sugar

3 tablespoons mild-flavored honey

1. POUR the vinegar into a saucepan and sprinkle the gelatin over it. Let the mixture stand briefly until the gelatin softens, about 5 minutes.

2. STIR in the sugar and warm the mixture over medium heat until steamy but short of boiling. Remove from the heat and mix in the honey, stirring until melted. Pour the mixture into a loaf pan or other dish of similar size.

3. REFRIGERATE for several hours, until set. The jelly is ready to use, or it can be kept refrigerated for up to a week. Slice it into cubes or other shapes and serve with grilled lamb, venison, or rabbit.

spicing **TIP** **Whenever we call for inexpensive balsamic vinegar, that means that the recipe doesn't require one aged for thirty-plus years that would cost a day's or week's paycheck. Try, however, to find one that is made of grape "must" as the first ingredient—and the less other stuff in it, the better. True Aceto Balsamico Tradizionale comes from the neighboring towns of Modena and Reggio Emilia in Italy, and is made of Trebbiano grapes that are aged in successively smaller wooden barrels over many years. Yours doesn't have to be *tradizionale*, but try to avoid added cara-**

mel color and guar gum or other things not related to grapes. Oleaceae, an oil and vinegar store in Santa Fe, offers a wonderful selection of options. They also carry Edmond Fallot Green Peppercorn Dijon Mustard, one of the best true Dijons on earth. Their products are available online from oleaceaeoliveoil.com. If you bump into us at the brick-and-mortar shop, please don't ask us how to pronounce the name.

CILANTRO-MINT CHUTNEY

FOR CONTEMPORARY SMOKED FOOD & GRILLED DISHES

This type of chutney sits on the tables of many Indian restaurants for spooning over all kinds of foods. We like it best with lamb, perhaps chops or kebabs with a slight Indian accent, such as ones glazed with Curry in a Hurry Baste (page 221). MAKES ABOUT 1 CUP

1 cup packed fresh cilantro leaves and tender stems
1 cup packed fresh mint leaves and tender stems
1 fresh serrano chile, seeded and chopped
1/4 cup water
1 tablespoon fresh lime juice
2 teaspoons minced fresh ginger
1/2 teaspoon granulated sugar
Kosher salt or coarse sea salt

1. **COMBINE** all of the ingredients in a food processor and puree the mixture.

2. **SERVE** the chutney right away with lamb. Refrigerate leftovers in a covered container for up to several days, but bring back to room temperature before serving again.

TAPENADE WITH GREEN OLIVES AND WALNUTS

FOR GRILLED DISHES

We had the great fortune to lead culinary adventures in France's Dordogne region for more than a decade. Walnuts flourish in the area, and we used to scavenge them from our friend Wendely's grove of trees. The slight astringency of the walnuts pairs perfectly with the tang of green olives. The flavor gets a little muddied by smoke, though, so we reserve the combo for grilled rabbit, lamb chops, or leg of lamb. **MAKES ABOUT 2 CUPS**

1 scant cup walnut pieces

1 cup pitted briny green olives

2 tablespoons unsalted butter, softened

1 to 2 teaspoons Armagnac or brandy

$1/2$ teaspoon Dijon mustard

1 or 2 anchovy fillets

3 to 4 tablespoons olive oil

1. TOAST the walnut pieces in a small, heavy skillet over medium-low heat just until fragrant. Dump the walnuts into a food processor and add the olives, butter, Armagnac, mustard, and anchovies. Pulse several times to chop and combine into a roughly textured mixture. With the processor running, pour in the oil in a steady stream, using just enough oil to sufficiently bind the tapenade into a glistening, coarse puree.

2. SCRAPE the tapenade into a small bowl. Let sit for about 30 minutes for the flavors to mingle before serving. If you want to hold the tapenade for a longer time, store it in a covered container in the refrigerator and bring it back to room temperature before serving with grilled meat.

GIN-POACHED DRIED CHERRIES WITH JUNIPER BERRIES

FOR CONTEMPORARY SMOKED FOOD & GRILLED DISHES

Another fruit accompaniment, but with a boozy element to boot. We chose gin because it often has juniper berries in the mix of botanicals that flavor it. Juniper berries especially enhance lamb and game meats. **MAKES ABOUT 2 CUPS**

> 3/4 cup water
> 1/4 cup gin
> 1/2 cup granulated sugar
> 8 juniper berries, bruised with a wooden spoon
> 1 bay leaf
> 1/4 teaspoon dried thyme
> 1 1/4 cups dried cherries

1. COMBINE the water, gin, sugar, juniper berries, bay leaf, and thyme in a small saucepan. Bring the mixture to a quick boil over medium-high heat, then reduce the heat to a simmer and cook for 5 minutes, for the flavors to blend somewhat. Stir in the cherries and continue to cook for 8 minutes more. Remove the pan from the heat and let stand for at least 15 minutes for the cherries to further soak up the flavorful liquid.

2. SERVE warm or chilled with lamb or venison. The cherry mixture will keep in a covered container in the refrigerator for up to 3 weeks.

spicing TIP Juniper berries are not true berries, but they do come from juniper shrubs. They are picked when they have turned bluish in color. Bruising them by giving them a few whacks with a wooden spoon releases more of their rosemary-and-pine–like fragrance. The berries, which also have a slight acidity, are a classic match with venison, rabbit, pheasant, and squab. You can find them in the various spice lines sold at supermarkets, but the berries we have ordered from penzeys.com have been especially robust. Penzeys also now has some 70 retail stores.

PISTACHIO-MINT PESTO

FOR GRILLED DISHES

Just outside of Alamogordo, New Mexico, sits one of those iconic roadside attractions, "The World's Largest Pistachio Nut," heralding your arrival to McGinn's Pistachio Tree Ranch. You don't really need to know that to enjoy this recipe, but if you're ever in the neighborhood, you should stop for a look and pick up some tasty nuts, too. Pistachios yield scrumptious creaminess when turned into pesto, like this one crafted to accompany lamb, venison, or rabbit. You only need a big spoonful per serving. **MAKES ABOUT 2 CUPS**

1 cup shelled unsalted pistachios
1 cup packed fresh mint leaves
1 garlic clove
1 tablespoon fresh lemon juice
3/4 cup olive oil
1/2 teaspoon crushed hot red chile flakes
1/2 teaspoon kosher salt or coarse sea salt, or more to taste

1. PLACE the pistachios, mint, and garlic in a food processor. Process until finely chopped. With the processor running, pour in the lemon juice and then the oil in a slow, steady stream. When well combined, add the chiles and salt and process again. Taste to see if more salt is needed.

2. USE THE pesto at room temperature, spooned over lamb, venison, or rabbit. To store leftovers, top with a thin film of additional olive oil, cover, and refrigerate for up to 3 weeks.

VARIATION: Trade out pistachios for almonds if you wish, but the McGinn family won't like it.

PEPERONCINI, CUCUMBER, AND RICOTTA SALATA RELISH

FOR TRADITIONAL BARBECUE, CONTEMPORARY SMOKED FOOD, & GRILLED DISHES

For a more rustic preparation of lamb or young goat, sliced or pulled, we like this assertive mix, part salad, part relish, and totally delightful. The idea came to us when we ordered a chopped salad at our local neighborhood market, Kaune's, in Santa Fe. The peperoncini used here are the pickled yellow-green peppers available in jars alongside other pickles. The ricotta salata cheese included is typically sheep's milk cheese that has been salted, pressed, and aged for about three months. The cheese's texture is dense but a touch spongy, and it can be grated into a dish or broken into crumbles, which we favor here. We think the relish is at its best when served shortly after preparing it. MAKES ABOUT 2³/₄ CUPS

1 cup chopped drained pickled peperoncini peppers
1 cup chopped, peeled, seeded cucumber
2 tablespoons minced fresh flat-leaf parsley
1 tablespoon olive oil
¹/₂ teaspoon kosher salt or coarse sea salt
³/₄ cup crumbled ricotta salata cheese

1. STIR together the peperoncini, cucumber, parsley, oil, and salt in a bowl. Combine well.

2. ADD the cheese to the bowl and toss lightly to combine. Spoon at room temperature onto pulled lamb or goat sandwiches, or just serve as an accompaniment to slices of either meat.

VARIATION: If you want a little heat in this, chop up a few small red Calabrian chiles (generally packaged in oil) or add a sprinkling of crushed hot red chile flakes.

WILD MUSHROOM COMPOTE

Whether your mushrooms come from the wild or from the corner grocery store, this compote is tastiest with spring morels or fall porcinis or chanterelles, but even button mushrooms come to life in this simple but rich treatment. Serve it with grilled or smoked rack of lamb, rabbit, or any cut of venison. Minus the coriander, the compote makes a good accompaniment to beefy steaks as well. We prefer it made shortly before serving. MAKES ABOUT 2 CUPS

> 4 bacon slices, chopped
> 2 tablespoons unsalted butter
> 1 pound mushrooms, preferably wild, thinly sliced
> 1 shallot, minced
> 1/4 teaspoon ground coriander
> Kosher salt or coarse sea salt
> 2 tablespoons dry red wine

1. FRY the bacon in a heavy skillet over medium heat until brown and crisp, 8 to 10 minutes. Remove the bacon from the skillet with a slotted spoon, drain on paper towels, and reserve.

2. MELT the butter in the bacon drippings in the skillet. Stir in the mushrooms, shallot, coriander, and salt to taste. The mushrooms will give up a good bit of liquid. Stir occasionally and continue to cook until the liquid has nearly evaporated.

3. STIR in the wine and reserved bacon, stir again a few times, and remove from the heat. Serve warm with lamb, venison, or rabbit.

VEGETABLE
LOVE

DRY RUBS, PASTES, AND MARINADES

SMOKY SWEET PAPRIKA RUB

FOR CONTEMPORARY SMOKED FOOD & GRILLED DISHES

A little smoke and a little sweetness add vibrancy to carrots grilled in a wire basket or smoked eggplant or onion slices. **MAKES ABOUT 1 CUP**

1/4 cup smoked sweet paprika

2 tablespoons dried mustard powder

2 tablespoons packed brown sugar

2 tablespoons kosher salt or coarse sea salt or smoked salt (see Spicing Tip, page 12)

1 tablespoon crumbled dried thyme

1 tablespoon garlic powder

1 tablespoon toasted ground cumin seed

1 tablespoon toasted ground coriander seed

1 tablespoon freshly ground black pepper

1. STIR together all of the ingredients in a bowl. Sprinkle the rub lightly on oil-sprayed vegetables just before cooking.

2. STORE any leftover rub in a covered container in a cool, dark pantry for up to 3 months.

spicing **TIP** Because vegetables generally cook quickly over the fire, they don't have much opportunity to soak up smoky flavors unless they are in a full-scale barbecue pit fired with wood logs. For that reason, we often rub or baste the vegetables with strongly smoke-flavored ingredients, items like smoked Spanish paprika, chipotle chiles, or smoked salt.

SMOKY ANCHO RUB

FOR CONTEMPORARY SMOKED FOOD & GRILLED DISHES

We like this rub on corn on the cob, onions or leeks, zucchini and other summer squash, portobello mushrooms, wedges of pumpkin or other winter squash, and small sweet potatoes. MAKES ABOUT 1 CUP

1/4 cup ground dried ancho chile

1/4 cup smoked sweet paprika

1/4 cup kosher salt or coarse sea salt

1 tablespoon smoked salt (see Spicing Tip, page 12) or additional kosher salt or coarse sea salt

2 teaspoons garlic powder

2 teaspoons onion powder

2 teaspoons celery salt

1. STIR together all of the ingredients in a bowl. Sprinkle the rub lightly on oil-sprayed vegetables just before cooking.

2. STORE any leftover rub in a covered container in a cool, dark pantry for up to 3 months.

spicing **TIP** Vegetables thrive on the grill and in the smoker. They taste super prepared outdoors, and never require long cooking times, even when slow-smoked. They grill best over steady medium heat, easy to manage on any type of grill. Best of all, vegetables are almost fully forgiving of any mistakes and they're done when you say they are, with no specific internal temperature needed for palatability or safety. We frequently use a "wet" seasoning method with vegetables on the grill or smoker, one including oil or butter in particular, because of the lack of fat in vegetables. Much of it drips away while cooking. If opting for a dry rub, we always spritz the surface with a vegetable oil spray.

OLIVE OIL AND ALLIUMS PASTE

Members of the onion family add some heft to this easy olive oil paste. Brush or rub it on vegetables with broad surfaces such as quartered heads of fennel or radicchio, or slices of summer squash, onion, eggplant, potatoes, portly mushrooms, and multi-hued bell peppers. MAKES ABOUT 1/2 CUP

> 1/2 cup olive oil
> 1 shallot, cut in several chunks
> 2 garlic cloves
> 3/4 teaspoon kosher salt or coarse sea salt, or more to taste
> 1/4 teaspoon freshly ground black pepper

1. **PLACE** all of the ingredients in a food processor or blender and puree. Massage the mixture on the cut surfaces of vegetables.

2. **ALLOW** the seasoned vegetables to sit for at least 10 minutes at room temperature prior to cooking. Refrigerate any leftover paste in a covered container for up to a week.

VARIATION: Add chopped capers, or minced fresh thyme, marjoram, basil, or oregano leaves, to the paste.

spicing TIP **If you have nothing in your pantry but a bottle of olive oil and a box of salt, you can whip together endless platters of grilled or smoked vegetables. From the season's first scrumptious asparagus to those end-of-season winter squashes, nothing else is really necessary for flavoring. We go further in our recipes to diversify the options, but simplicity often works splendidly.**

SOY MARINADE

FOR CONTEMPORARY SMOKED FOOD & GRILLED DISHES

Marinades in general work better with meat and seafood than with vegetables, which can get soggy quickly. An important exception for us is the opportunity to add soy sauce flavor in a short bath to eggplant rounds, portobello mushroom slices, asparagus, and baby onions on the stem before grilling or lightly smoking, or to tofu and tempeh before grilling. MAKES ABOUT 1 CUP

> 1/2 cup soy sauce
> 1/4 cup mirin
> 1 tablespoon peanut or vegetable oil
> 1 tablespoon minced fresh ginger
> 2 teaspoons Asian sesame oil
> 2 garlic cloves, minced

1. WHISK together all of the ingredients in a bowl or combine them in a large zipper-lock plastic bag. Use the marinade right away or cover and refrigerate it for up to a couple of days.

2. POUR the marinade over the vegetables and let sit for about 15 minutes at room temperature prior to cooking.

MOPS AND BASTES

OLD BAY BASTE

FOR CONTEMPORARY SMOKED FOOD & GRILLED DISHES

We like to brush this on ears of corn, thick onion rings, potato wedges or small whole potatoes, and small artichokes. Old Bay, the esteemed Maryland seafood seasoning in the bright yellow and blue can, seems to be in just about every supermarket we've visited. With this baste, you'll need no further seasoning before cooking or at the table. As you might guess, blue crabs will lap this up, too. **MAKES ABOUT ⅔ CUP**

> 8 tablespoons (1 stick) unsalted butter
> 2 to 3 teaspoons Old Bay Seasoning
> Minced zest and juice of 1 medium lemon

1. **MELT** the butter in a small saucepan and stir in the other ingredients. Keep warm and baste on vegetables two or three times while cooking.

2. **LEFTOVERS** can be refrigerated in a covered container and kept for up to a week. Reheat the baste before using it again.

VARIATION: If you happen to be popping open some bottles of brew, share a few splashes of beer with the baste, from a couple of tablespoons up to ⅓ cup, as you wish.

SHERRY VINEGAR BASTE

FOR GRILLED DISHES

Sherry vinegar is aged Spanish vinegar made from—obviously—sherry. The vinegar is dark and potent but also smooth and rounded, with a hint of sweetness. Any store that sells quality vinegars and oils should stock it. The baste stokes the flavor of vegetables seasoned in advance with Smoky Sweet Paprika Rub (page 246) or Olive Oil and Alliums Paste (page 248).

MAKES ABOUT 3/4 CUP

> 1/3 cup sherry vinegar
>
> 1/3 cup water, vegetable stock, or chicken stock
>
> 3 tablespoons olive oil
>
> 2 teaspoons compatible dry rub or seasoning paste, optional, or 1 teaspoon kosher salt or coarse sea salt

1. WARM all of the ingredients in a small saucepan. Keep warm and baste on vegetables twice, once at the beginning and again near the end of the grilling process.

2. LEFTOVERS can be refrigerated in a covered container and kept for up to a week. Reheat the baste before using it again.

CHIPOTLE, LIME, AND SHALLOT VINAIGRETTE

FOR CONTEMPORARY SMOKED FOOD & GRILLED DISHES

This citrus- and chile-spiked dressing shouts "Party Time!" for tomatoes, corn, onions, sweet potatoes, or bell peppers. MAKES ABOUT 1 CUP

> 1 tablespoon white vinegar
> 1 teaspoon freshly grated lime zest plus 1/4 cup fresh lime juice
> 1 small shallot, minced
> 1/2 cup olive oil
> 1 canned chipotle chile, minced, plus 2 tablespoons adobo sauce from the can
> Kosher salt or coarse sea salt
> Freshly ground black pepper

1. WHISK together the vinegar, lime zest and lime juice, and shallot in a bowl. Let the mixture stand for 10 minutes.

2. WHISK in the oil, add the chipotle and adobo sauce, and season to taste with salt and pepper. Serve right away at the table to spoon over vegetables.

SOY, MISO, AND GINGER DRESSING

FOR GRILLED DISHES

Miso, the fermented soybean paste, gives body to this Japanese-inspired dressing, making it appropriate for brushing on vegetables while they are cooking as well as when they are served at the table. Try it on halves of long, slim Asian eggplants, on regular eggplant slices, or on mushrooms, perhaps first zipped up with Soy Marinade (page 249). You can also paint this on onion, zucchini, and yellow squash slices on the grill or tableside. As a bonus, it's a good glaze for grilled scallops, too. MAKES ABOUT 1 CUP

1/2 cup vegetable oil or sunflower oil

1/4 cup soy sauce

2 tablespoons white miso paste

1 tablespoon rice vinegar

1 tablespoon Asian sesame oil

2 teaspoons brown sugar

Walnut-sized chunk of fresh ginger, minced

1 garlic clove, minced

1/4 teaspoon ground white pepper

1. WHISK together all of the ingredients in a small bowl. Brush or drizzle the mixture over vegetables once while you're grilling them and then again at the table.

2. REFRIGERATED in a covered container, the sauce will keep for up to a week.

ORANGE-HAZELNUT VINAIGRETTE

FOR GRILLED DISHES

Classic barbecue sauces, whether based on tomatoes, mustard, or vinegar, don't do much to enhance vegetables. Mustard and vinegar work well only as team players along with oil, as in this vinaigrette. We love the subtleties of hazelnut oil here on grilled vegetables such as asparagus, endive, radicchio, fennel, and broccoli. The vinaigrette is best made up shortly before serving.

MAKES ABOUT 1 CUP

> 2 tablespoons Champagne vinegar or rice vinegar
>
> 2 teaspoons freshly grated orange zest plus 1/4 cup fresh orange juice
>
> 1/2 teaspoon Dijon mustard
>
> 1/4 cup plus 2 tablespoons hazelnut oil
>
> 1/4 cup vegetable oil or sunflower oil
>
> 2 tablespoons chopped toasted hazelnuts
>
> Kosher salt or coarse sea salt
>
> Ground white pepper

1. WHISK together the vinegar, orange zest and orange juice, and mustard in a bowl.

2. WHISK in both of the oils, add the nuts, and season to taste with salt and white pepper. Serve right away at the table to spoon over grilled vegetables.

VARIATION: Radicchio and endive have a pleasant bitterness about them, which makes them candidates for a sweeter dressing, too. For a balsamic orange vinaigrette, replace the Champagne vinegar with balsamic and the hazelnut oil with olive oil. Increase the Dijon mustard to 1 1/2 teaspoons.

SPICY HUMMUS SAUCE

FOR GRILLED DISHES

Hot sauce and some greens contribute color and luster to this hummus mixture. We prefer it pooled under bright peppers, zucchini, and halved plum tomatoes cooked on the grill. MAKES ABOUT 2 CUPS

1/4 cup extra-virgin olive oil

4 garlic cloves, peeled and roasted in a dry skillet until soft

14- to-15-ounce can chickpeas, rinsed and drained

Grated zest of 1 lemon plus 3 tablespoons fresh lemon juice

2 tablespoons minced fresh mint or a combination of mint and parsley or dill

1 tablespoon tahini (sesame butter)

1 tablespoon red chile–based hot sauce or harissa

Kosher salt or coarse sea salt

1. PUREE the olive oil and garlic in a food processor. When smooth, add the chickpeas, lemon zest and juice, mint, tahini, and hot sauce, and puree. Taste and season with salt. If the mixture is too thick to spoon easily, add a tablespoon or three of water, until it reaches that stage.

2. SERVE the sauce right away with grilled vegetables. Refrigerate any remaining sauce in a covered container for up to 5 days, but allow it to come back to room temperature before serving again. It may also require a bit more water to thin after refrigeration.

spicing **TIP** **In our rather mad condiment experimentation while working on this book, we discovered BLiS Blast Bourbon Barrel-Aged Hot Pepper Sauce, from food52.com/provisions. It's aged in casks that have housed bourbon, as you might guess, but the barrels also aged stout beer. The sauce is great on a burger or steak and remarkably good in this sauce and on vegetables. Hot but not scorching, it allows nuances of wood, bourbon, vanilla, and hops to come through distinctly.**

BLOOD ORANGE MAYONNAISE

FOR GRILLED DISHES

The deep garnet juice of the late winter blood orange makes a startlingly beautiful mayonnaise. It can accompany chilled grilled leeks or grilled asparagus, green beans, or zucchini. If it's not the season for blood oranges, use any other orange or tangerine. **MAKES ABOUT 1 CUP**

2/3 cup mayonnaise
1 tablespoon extra-virgin olive oil
1 teaspoon freshly grated blood orange zest plus 1/4 cup fresh blood orange juice
Pinch of kosher salt or coarse sea salt

1. WHISK together all of the ingredients in a small bowl.

2. SPOON a small amount over or alongside vegetables at the table. Refrigerate leftovers in a covered container for up to 3 days.

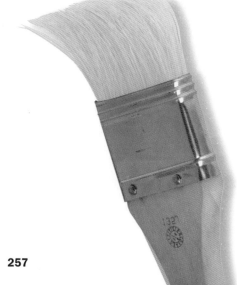

CHILE-SCENTED BROWN BUTTER

FOR GRILLED DISHES

The aroma of butter browning is almost as scrumptious as bread baking. Browning the milk solids contributes a toasty element. This butter is an especially fine finish for grilled ears of corn, sweet onion halves or slices, potato slices or wedges, or tomato halves. The chile adds just a hint of flavor to complement the butter's richness. **MAKES ABOUT ¹/₂ CUP**

8 tablespoons (1 stick) unsalted butter
¹/₂ teaspoon mild ground red chile, such as New Mexican
Pinch or two of salt, optional

1. IF YOU have a choice, pick a shallow saucepan with a light-colored bottom so that you can easily see the change in color that will occur in the butter. Place the butter in the pan and warm over medium heat. Swirl the pan around a bit as the butter melts and bubbles. The water in the butter must first evaporate, then the milk solids will turn golden and, finally, a nice medium brown.

2. REMOVE from the heat immediately (the butter can easily burn if you're not watching closely), add the chile and salt, if you wish, and pour into a heatproof container to stop the cooking. Use the butter right away, brushed over vegetables. Just a little is needed to yield big flavor.

spicing **TIP** The Indian cooking fat known as ghee is clarified butter, made by removing the milk solids. The version from Ancient Organics has an especially toasty taste and features our favorite nationally available organic butter, from Straus Family Creamery. Just warm the ghee, toss in a clove or two of garlic and the ground chile, and you will be ready to go with a twist on this recipe. You can order it online at ancientorganics.com.

OTHER CONDIMENTS FOR FLAVORING

ALMOND, SAGE, AND CELERY RELISH

The fall flavors in this relish nicely complement later-season vegetables such as sweet potatoes, pumpkin, and winter squash. The contrasting textural crunch provides an extra bonus. **MAKES ABOUT 3/4 CUP**

> 1/2 cup roasted, salted Marcona almonds, coarsely chopped
> 1/4 cup minced celery ribs
> 2 to 3 tablespoons chopped fresh sage
> 2 tablespoons chopped celery leaves or fresh flat-leaf parsley
> 2 teaspoons olive oil

1. **STIR** together all of the ingredients in a small bowl.

2. **THE MIXTURE** can sit for 1 hour or so at room temperature before serving spooned alongside vegetables.

FRESH TOMATO RELISH

FOR CONTEMPORARY SMOKED FOOD & GRILLED DISHES

Make this as colorful as you wish with summer tomatoes in rainbow hues, but please use real garden or farmers' market tomatoes. If you want to give the relish more heft, so that a vegetable platter can be the centerpiece of a meal, mix in some cooked Israeli couscous, black beans, or a grain like farro. As an accompaniment without other added ingredients, spoon it over grilled or smoked eggplant, onions, or fennel. The relish is at its peak just after you put it together, so eat up. MAKES ABOUT 2 CUPS

> 2 cups mixed chopped tomatoes, big and small varieties
> About 2 tablespoons extra-virgin olive oil
> Splash of white vinegar
> A few fresh basil leaves
> Flaky salt, such as Maldon, or kosher salt or coarse sea salt

1. COMBINE the tomatoes in a bowl with the oil and vinegar. The mixture can sit for 1 hour at room temperature, but don't refrigerate it.

2. JUST BEFORE serving over vegetables at the table, tear the basil leaves into small bits and scatter them on the relish. Season generously with salt and serve.

VARIATION: Transform this into a caprese relish, and make it a bit more substantial, by adding torn chunks of mozzarella.

spicing **TIP** **A final flourish of certain cheeses can up the pizzazz of outdoor cooked foods. Grated Parmesan or Pecorino, or Mexican-style queso fresco or aged Cotija, are tasty on corn, onions, eggplant, and more.**

CAPONATA

This Sicilian vegetable relish can enhance simply grilled versions of any of its key ingredients—eggplant, plum tomatoes, and bell peppers. It's great, too, accompanying grilled portobello mushroom caps or zucchini planks.

MAKES ABOUT 2 CUPS

$1/3$ cup olive oil

2 garlic cloves, minced

1 medium eggplant, cut in neat dice

1 medium red bell pepper, seeded and cut in neat dice

2 medium red-ripe plum tomatoes, cut in neat dice

1 teaspoon kosher salt or coarse sea salt, or more to taste

2 tablespoons capers, chopped if large

2 peperoncini peppers, chopped

1 to 2 tablespoons red wine vinegar

1 teaspoon granulated sugar

1. WARM the oil over medium heat in a large skillet. Add the garlic and cook for 1 minute. Stir in the eggplant, bell pepper, tomatoes, and 1 teaspoon salt. Sauté until the vegetables have softened and have begun to give up their juices, about 10 minutes.

2. STIR in the capers, peperoncini, 1 tablespoon vinegar, and sugar and cook for another minute. Taste to see if more salt or vinegar is needed. The caponata may be used immediately or cooled and refrigerated in a covered container for up to 3 days. It can be served chilled, at room temperature, or hot, spooned over or alongside vegetables.

VARIATION: If you want to fire up a grill a bit ahead of time, grill the key caponata ingredients. Instead of beginning with diced eggplant, pepper, and tomatoes, slice the eggplant $1/2$ inch thick and halve the tomatoes lengthwise. Oil them and the whole pepper and grill over medium heat until each is tender. Then dice and continue the recipe, but sauté the mixture together for only about 3 minutes.

LUSCIOUS FRUIT

DRY RUBS, PASTES, AND MARINADES

RED MAPLE SUGAR

Adding sugar to fruit destined for the grill or smoker helps caramelize the natural sugars. As with vegetables, it's a good idea to give fruit a spritz of oil before cooking, to prevent it from sticking to the cooking grate and also to ensure that a dry spice mixture will adhere. We especially like this rub on grilled watermelon, cantaloupe, and apple slices served for dessert.

MAKES ABOUT 1/2 CUP

1/2 cup coarse-ground maple sugar
1 teaspoon ground dried mild red chile, such as New Mexican
1/4 teaspoon ground dried mace or freshly grated nutmeg
Pinch of fine sea salt

1. STIR together all of the ingredients in a small bowl. Sprinkle heavily over oil-spritzed fruit prior to cooking.

2. ANY REMAINING rub can be stored in a covered container in a cool, dry pantry for up to 3 months.

SWEET AND NUTTY OIL

FOR GRILLED DISHES

We like this simple paste best on grilled fruit, perhaps banana, peach, or plum halves, or apple, pineapple, mango, or pear slices. Stir it up just before you want to cook the fruit. Be sure to grill fruit over a medium to medium-low fire, so that it softens and gets a few caramelized edges before it burns. That makes fruit perfect for grilling as dessert after a main dish, when the grill is cooling down. **MAKES ABOUT 1/2 CUP**

> 1/3 cup almond, walnut, or macadamia nut oil
>
> 2 tablespoons turbinado sugar
>
> 1/8 teaspoon ground cinnamon

1. **STIR** together all of the ingredients in a small bowl.

2. **BRUSH** the mixture over the fruit halves or slices before grilling them.

VARIATION: Melted bacon drippings or lard can substitute for the oil. This twist is ridiculously good on grilled apples and peaches. Of course, you can also opt for melted butter as another tasty fat.

spicing **TIP** Smoked cinnamon can be a transcendent spice and would be a fabulous ingredient here instead of regular ground cinnamon. We've tried smoking our own but haven't been thrilled with the result. However, Lior Lev Sercarz, master of all things spice, offers a superlative smoked cinnamon at his La Boîte shop in New York City or online (laboiteny.com). It's called Smoked Cinnamon N.18. Try it also in barbecue sauces for pork ribs or pulled pork, perhaps our Sweet Coffee-Cascabel Sauce (page 39) or Aliño (page 14). Also consider Lior's other remarkable spice blends, mixtures that chefs such as Eric Ripert and Daniel Boulud have been using for years. We first came across Lior's spices and blends at Sofra, Chef Ana Sortun's entrancing Middle Eastern–inspired bakery in Cambridge, Massachusetts.

PIÑA COLADA MARINADE

FOR GRILLED DISHES

How about a piña colada on a plate? Use this marinade to zest up and caramelize pineapple spears, or halved bananas, peaches, or nectarines. For extra punch, toast some shredded coconut in a dry skillet on the grill and sprinkle it over the fruit just before serving. **MAKES ABOUT 1 CUP**

> 1/2 cup light, dark, or spiced rum
> 1/2 cup unsweetened pineapple juice
> 2 tablespoons canned cream of coconut, such as Coco Lopez
> 2 teaspoons vegetable oil or sunflower oil

1. WHISK together all of the ingredients in a small bowl.

2. POUR the mixture over fruit and marinate at room temperature for about 15 minutes prior to cooking.

spicing **TIP** Various complementary fruit juices and nectars can be used to moisten fruit destined for the grill. Among the many options, we particularly like *verjus* (or verjuice), a refreshingly tart grape juice often made by wineries, and sold in some retail stores and online. The sweeter and more syrupy the juice, the more you may want to balance it with a little neutral vegetable oil or melted butter.

MOPS AND BASTES

FRUITY VINEGAR BASTE

FOR CONTEMPORARY SMOKED FOOD & GRILLED DISHES

For this baste, pick a fruit juice blend that you think will be compatible with the fruit you are grilling or smoking. We suggest a few options below, but the array of choices seems to expand daily. MAKES ABOUT 1¼ CUPS

1 cup fruit juice cocktail, such as white grape–peach, guava-pineapple, or strawberry-peach

1/4 cup fruit vinegar, such as raspberry

2 tablespoons unsalted butter

Pinch of ground cayenne, optional

1. **WARM** all of the ingredients in a small saucepan.

2. **KEEP THE** mixture warm and baste on fruit two or three times while cooking. Leftovers can be refrigerated in a covered container for up to a week. Reheat the baste before using it again.

SWEETLY SAVORY FRUIT BASTE

FOR GRILLED DISHES

We aren't big on achingly sweet finishes to meals, so we love the number of restaurant desserts that incorporate savory elements these days. This baste keeps fruit moist while it cooks, but also imparts herbal and olive notes. To boost the overall seasoning, sprinkle the fruit first with Red Maple Sugar (page 264). **MAKES ABOUT 1¼ CUPS**

> 1 cup unsweetened white grape juice
>
> ¼ cup olive oil
>
> 1 tablespoon minced fresh lemon verbena, lemon thyme, or mint, or a combination
>
> ½ teaspoon kosher salt or coarse sea salt

1. WARM all of the ingredients in a small saucepan.

2. KEEP THE mixture warm and baste on fruit once near the end of the grilling process. Leftovers can be refrigerated in a covered container for up to a week.

SAUCES

SAFFRON-HONEY BUTTER

FOR GRILLED DISHES

After discovering bottles of saffron syrup at our local branch of the Spanish Table, we started playing around with the extraordinary spice in desserts rather than just in savory preparations. This recipe doesn't use the syrup, but was inspired by it. Brush it on grilled figs, pears, mangoes, or pineapple.

MAKES ABOUT 1/2 CUP

> 8 tablespoons (1 stick) unsalted butter
> 1 tablespoon mild-flavored honey
> 2 big pinches of saffron threads

1. MELT the butter in a small saucepan over medium-low heat. Stir in the honey and saffron.

2. WHEN THE honey has melted into the butter and the saffron has "bloomed" red-yellow, the butter is ready. Serve right away, spooned on grilled fruit.

TANGY DULCE DE LECHE

FOR GRILLED DISHES

Dulce de leche, milk jam, confiture de lait, and cajeta are just a few of the world's versions of milk cooked down with sugar into an addictive sauce. By any name, we'll eat it directly off a spoon, but with a little luck some will be left to accompany grilled pineapple or peaches or bananas. The tang in this recipe comes from goat's milk. For a milder version you can substitute regular whole cow's milk. This sauce has a fair bit of salt for fans of salted caramel like us, but you can leave that out if you wish. MAKES ABOUT 1 CUP

    1 quart goat's milk

    1 cup granulated sugar

    1 tablespoon light corn syrup

    1 vanilla bean, split lengthwise and seeds scraped

    1 teaspoon kosher salt or coarse sea salt, optional

1. COMBINE the milk, sugar, corn syrup, vanilla bean and scrapings, and, if you like, salt in a large, heavy saucepan. Bring to a boil over medium heat, then reduce the heat to a low simmer. Cook until deeply golden brown and thick and reduced to about 1 cup, 50 to 60 minutes, stirring frequently toward the end.

2. SERVE the dulce de leche immediately, spooned warm over grilled fruit. You can also cool and store the sauce in a covered container in the refrigerator for up to 3 weeks, but reheat it before using.

LIME-CAYENNE DESSERT SYRUP

FOR GRILLED DISHES

We infuse a basic cocktail syrup here with a little spark. Try this one on grilled mango or papaya slices or kebabs. MAKES ABOUT 2 CUPS

> 1 cup granulated sugar
> 1 cup water
> 3 or 4 dried cayenne chiles
> Zest (in strips) and juice of 3 medium limes

1. COMBINE the sugar, water, and chiles in a small saucepan. Bring to a boil over medium heat, stirring a few times to dissolve the sugar. Add the lime zest and juice and remove from the heat. Steep the mixture for 20 to 30 minutes.

2. POUR the mixture through a fine-mesh strainer into a jar or bottle. Use the syrup right away, brushed over fruit when it's served at the table. You can store leftover syrup in a covered container in the refrigerator for up to a month. The flavor gradually fades over time.

> **VARIATION:** For lime-mint syrup, eliminate the chiles and add a handful of fresh mint leaves along with the lime zest and juice. Use your imagination for other combos of fruit and herbs in syrup.

SANGRIA SAUCE

FOR GRILLED DISHES

We created a sauce similar to this for a Spanish-themed grill meal for *Eating Well* magazine. It adds a little flamenco-like spirit to grilled peaches, nectarines, or pears, or even grill-toasted slices of angel food cake. MAKES ABOUT 1½ CUPS

> 1½ cups fruity red wine
> 6-ounce can frozen orange juice concentrate, thawed
> 3 tablespoons Cointreau or Triple Sec
> 3 tablespoons brandy
> 1 to 2 tablespoons granulated sugar
> 2 teaspoons fresh lemon juice

1. COMBINE the wine, juice concentrate, Cointreau, brandy, and 1 tablespoon sugar in a saucepan and bring to a boil over high heat. Reduce the heat to medium-low and simmer until reduced by about one-third. Taste and add more sugar if you wish, cooking an additional few minutes until dissolved.

2. SERVE the sauce warm to spoon over grilled fruit. You can also cool and store the sauce in a covered container in the refrigerator for up to a week, but reheat it before using.

> VARIATION: If you want to get a touch more ambitious, fire up the grill early and grill some orange slices for the sauce. Spray thin orange slices with oil, then grill them over medium heat just long enough to soften and get a little char in a few spots. Add the slices to the sauce, and see that each diner gets one when you pour the mixture over other fruit.

spicing **TIP** Fruit-infused vinegars make fine flavoring agents for grilled or smoked fruit. To make your own, put 1 pound of raspberries, strawberries, or other berries or stone fruit such as cherries or peaches in a saucepan. Add 1½ cups white vinegar and lightly mash the fruit. Add 1 tablespoon granulated sugar. Bring the mixture just to a boil, stirring to dissolve the sugar. Pour it all into a large sterilized jar or bowl and cover.

Let the mixture steep for about 2 weeks, shaking or stirring it around each day. Strain out the fruit and discard it. Pour the vinegar through a fine-mesh strainer and then pour into a sterilized bottle or bottles. For optimum flavor, use within a few months. Drizzle a bit over grilled or smoked fruit or grilled pound cake. The vinegar can be used in many salad dressings, too.

GINGERED CRÈME FRAÎCHE

FOR CONTEMPORARY SMOKED FOOD & GRILLED DISHES

Softly whipped cream can be a fine "sauce" for grilled or even smoked fruit. We tend to prefer the extra acidity of velvety crème fraîche ourselves. You can buy it and then stir in a bit of spice, but it's a snap to make yourself—and cheaper than store-bought versions. Avoid ultra-pasteurized cream, which has been heated high enough to blast it of good as well as bad bacteria. You need some of those good ones to get the cream to culture, which is an overnight task. **MAKES ABOUT 1¼ CUPS**

> 1 cup whipping cream, not a variety that has been ultra-pasteurized
> 3 tablespoons buttermilk or plain yogurt with active cultures
> 1 tablespoon packed brown sugar
> ½ teaspoon ground dried ginger
> 2 tablespoons minced crystallized ginger

1. STIR together the cream and buttermilk in a bowl. Cover it loosely and set it in a warm place in the kitchen for at least 8 hours and up to 12 hours. The cream will thicken.

2. STIR in the brown sugar, ground ginger, and crystallized ginger. Refrigerate in a covered container for at least 1 hour before serving alongside fruit. The crème fraîche will keep for at least a week in the refrigerator if you can avoid the temptation to snack on it.

OTHER CONDIMENTS FOR FLAVORING

SMOKED WALNUTS

FOR GRILLED DISHES

We wouldn't fire up a big smoker to smoke some nuts, but if we have it going anyway we often slip in a tray of these. At other times we use our stovetop smoker, which works great for this quick task. We have always enjoyed smoked nuts as an appetizer, but it didn't occur to us until recently that they make a superb condiment for sprinkling over grilled fruit such as figs, pears, peaches, apricots, and apples. **MAKES ABOUT 1 CUP**

1 tablespoon unsalted butter
1 scant tablespoon packed brown sugar
1 teaspoon lightly crushed dried rosemary or $1^1/2$ teaspoons crumbled dried thyme
1 cup walnut halves
$1/2$ teaspoon kosher salt or coarse sea salt, or more to taste

1. PREPARE a smoker, bringing the temperature to 200°F to 220°F. A stovetop smoker will cook a good bit hotter, around 300°F, so adjust the cooking time accordingly.

2. MELT the butter with the brown sugar and rosemary in a skillet over medium-low heat. Stir in the walnuts, coating them well with the butter mixture. Stir in the salt, tasting as you add it.

3. TRANSFER the nut mixture to a shallow smoke-proof dish or piece of heavy-duty foil molded into a tray just large enough to hold the nuts in a single layer. Place the nuts in the smoker and cook until dried and fragrant, about 30 minutes. Transfer the nuts to a paper towel to cool. Use the nuts immediately, sprinkled lightly over grilled fruit, or let cool and keep in a covered container in a cool, dark pantry for up to 3 days.

BACON TOFFEE

You will need a candy thermometer for this heavenly candy crunch. While you rummage around looking for it, find a heatproof rubber spatula and some parchment paper or a silicone baking sheet pan liner. Don't eat all the toffee before you grill the fruit that it will adorn—perhaps apple slices or pear wedges. MAKES SEVERAL CUPS OF LIGHTLY PACKED TOFFEE "SHARDS"

6 bacon slices, finely chopped
6 tablespoons (3/4 stick) unsalted butter
1 cup granulated sugar
1 cup water

1. LINE a baking sheet with parchment paper or a silicone baking mat.

2. FRY the chopped bacon in a heavy skillet until brown and crisp, 8 to 10 minutes. Remove the bacon bits with a slotted spoon and drain on a paper towel.

3. MEASURE 2 tablespoons of the bacon drippings and transfer them to a heavy saucepan. (Save the remaining drippings for another use.) Clamp a candy thermometer onto the saucepan. Add the butter, sugar, and water. Over medium heat, bring the mixture to a boil while stirring more or less constantly with a wooden spoon. Let the mixture boil away, turning golden, until it reaches 295°F to 298°F. Immediately stir in the bacon bits and remove the saucepan from the heat, then pour the toffee out onto the prepared baking sheet. Spread the toffee quickly with a rubber spatula to about a 1/4-inch thickness or until it becomes too thick to spread. Let the toffee cool and set up, 30 minutes to 1 hour.

4. BREAK the toffee into irregular pieces. For sprinkling over grilled fruit, you will want the pieces to be bite-size.

COCOA-ALMOND CRUMBS

FOR GRILLED DISHES

Our friend Chef Martín Rios uses lots of baked crumb mixtures to add contrasting flavors and crunch to desserts at his Restaurant Martín in Santa Fe. We know a good thing when we taste it. This particular crumb mixture contributes chocolaty, nutty elements to grilled pears, apples, or other favorite fruits. **MAKES ABOUT 1 CUP**

6 tablespoons (3/4 stick) unsalted butter, melted
3/4 cup almond flour or almond meal
6 tablespoons all-purpose flour
6 tablespoons granulated sugar
1/4 cup unsweetened cocoa powder
2 teaspoons espresso powder

1. PREHEAT the oven to 325°F.

2. STIR together all of the ingredients in a medium-size bowl. Spread the mixture on a rimmed baking sheet.

3. BAKE until the crumbs are dried and lightly crispy, 15 to 18 minutes, stirring once about halfway through the baking time. Remove from the baking sheet with a spatula and let the crumbs cool. The crumbs can top fruit immediately or will keep for up to 3 days in a covered container in a cool, dark pantry.

ACKNOWLEDGMENTS

WE'D LIKE TO RECOGNIZE the staff at The Harvard Common Press for turning our manuscript into the good-looking book you hold in your hands. Thank-Q to Virginia Downes, creative services manager; Gabriella Marks, photographer; Richard Oriolo, designer; Pat Jalbert-Levine, production editor; Karen Wise, copy editor; and—most of all—editor-in-chief Dan Rosenberg. Super-agent Doe Coover, thanks for always TCB.

MEASUREMENT EQUIVALENTS

PLEASE NOTE THAT ALL CONVERSIONS ARE APPROXIMATE.

LIQUID CONVERSIONS

U.S.	METRIC
1 tsp	5 ml
1 tbs	15 ml
2 tbs	30 ml
3 tbs	45 ml
1/4 cup	60 ml
1/3 cup	75 ml
1/3 cup + 1 tbs	90 ml
1/3 cup + 2 tbs	100 ml
1/2 cup	120 ml
2/3 cup	150 ml
3/4 cup	180 ml
3/4 cup + 2 tbs	200 ml
1 cup	240 ml
1 cup + 2 tbs	275 ml
1 1/4 cups	300 ml
1 1/3 cups	325 ml
1 1/2 cups	350 ml
1 2/3 cups	375 ml
1 3/4 cups	400 ml
1 3/4 cups + 2 tbs	450 ml
2 cups (1 pint)	475 ml
2 1/2 cups	600 ml
3 cups	720 ml
4 cups (1 quart)	945 ml
	(1,000 ml is 1 liter)

WEIGHT CONVERSIONS

U.S./U.K.	METRIC
1/2 oz	14 g
1 oz	28 g
1 1/2 oz	43 g
2 oz	57 g
2 1/2 oz	71 g
3 oz	85 g
3 1/2 oz	100 g
4 oz	113 g
5 oz	142 g
6 oz	170 g
7 oz	200 g
8 oz	227 g
9 oz	255 g
10 oz	284 g
11 oz	312 g
12 oz	340 g
13 oz	368 g
14 oz	400 g
15 oz	425 g
1 lb	454 g

OVEN TEMPERATURE CONVERSIONS

°F	GAS MARK	°C
250	1/2	120
275	1	140
300	2	150
325	3	165
350	4	180
375	5	190
400	6	200
425	7	220
450	8	230
475	9	240
500	10	260
550	Broil	290

INDEX

NOTE: Page references in *italics* indicate photographs.